Washington

The World Capital in
The American Century
1941-1990

Mark N. Ozer

ISBN: 978-1541124448

i

"Each of us are called and each to his own measure of capacity and each in his own vision to create this first great American century. ...to exert upon the world the full impact of our influence and for such purposes as we see fit" -- Henry R. Luce (February 1941)

"This conjunction of an immense military establishment and large arms industry is new to American experience...Our toil, resources and livelihood are all involved, so is the very structure of our society. In the councils of government, we must guard against the acquisition of unwanted influence...by the military-industrial complex. The potential for the disastrous rise of misplaced power exists and will persist."" -- Dwight Eisenhower January 17, 1961.

"We must take this opportunity to make our Capital a more inspiring place in which to live and work. ...It should be designed so as to set an example for the nation, and to take its place among the most attractive in the world." -- Lyndon Johnson 1965

Table of Contents

INTRODUCTION

Throughout its history, the national capital of the United States has grown with the growth of the country. After the turmoil of the Civil War, it came indeed to be a national capital. Like the American flag, it came to represent the country as a national shrine. After the turmoil of its industrialization, now a world power, it participated in redressing the balance of power by intervening in what was then called the "Great War." The second great crisis of the Depression once again increased the role of the federal government and its central government and its capital to rescue the economy as an epitome of enlightened liberal capitalism.

During that time, the problems unsolved, if not created, by the Treaty of Versailles once again intruded into the life of Washington DC. No longer could the neighboring seas protect the outside world from intruding into the life of the country. In 1941, the then very influential publisher Henry Luce published an article in *Life Magazine* on February 17th, calling upon the United States to recognize its importance as the dominant world power. The remainder of the 20th century was to be indeed "The American Century."

Washington DC was to become a world capital in what was to become that time of world sovereignty. The city of Washington came to reflect this new role as it had similarly reflected its earlier roles as the national capital and the national shrine. During the era starting in 1941 to 1992, it strode the world as the capital of the "free world." to reflect not only its mission to reflect its world power but to represent a set of principles that was felt to reflect its values. The mission of the country was not to establish, like British had in the previous century an American Empire, but to establish a more global and universal organism not limited by territorial boundaries. It was to represent the spirit of a constitutional republic and the epitome of enlightened capitalism.

The idea that the American presidency was a casualty of the Cold War was not something discussed in the corridors of the White House. FDR in his time was prepared to mobilize and share the products of a self-confident society. He asked for sacrifice from millions. He recognized the importance of engaging the public. The fruits of the Cold War were the secrecy it had generated; the "dirty tricks," it had justified; and the illusions it had propagated.

The civil rights crisis of the 1960s started with the long drawn out response to the effects of the Civil War. The withdrawal of the representatives of the secessionist states freed the former Whig Party members of Congress (now Republicans) to carry out the long pent up major non-military legislative program that would affect the development of the economy and politics of the next generation. It is this domestic non-military program that would be the blueprint for the coming age. The building of the transcontinental railroad, the organization of the Department of Agriculture and the start of the land grant college system are some of its hallmarks.

The issue of slavery was of course central. The crisis of the Civil War amplified the role of President Lincoln as commander in chief with subordination of the Supreme Court as exemplified by the *Dred Scott* decision. The Lincoln Administration had its crest in the 13th Amendment that abolished slavery. The 14th and 15th Amendments formed the basis for Reconstruction during the succeeding Grant Administration that eventually ended in 1876. The short-term impulse of Reconstruction had been replaced by the segregation of the South and the political system of white supremacy.

During the twelve years of the FDR presidency not one single piece of civil rights legislation was passed. The Democratic Southern caucus was a significant part of the Congressional Democratic majority that supported the New Deal. To avoid their antagonism, no effort was made to abolish the white primary in the South; or abolish the poll tax. Since 1933, eighty-three blacks had been lynched by white Southerners. Senator Wagner had offered an anti-lynching bill each year since 1934. White supremacy went to the core of "states rights." No southern incumbent below the Mason-Dixon Line wanted to be "outniggered" in a Democratic primary.

The Second World War was marked by the Great Migration of blacks off the land toward enfranchisement in the Northern industrial

2

cities while the Jim Crow system began even to change in the South. Black votes became increasingly available for maintaining the Democratic Party presidential majority.

FDR had sought to change the Democratic Party into a permanent progressive force; its urban base in the North was however hobbled by its other base in the South. It would be those same Southern Democrats who would provide the president bedrock support to resist aggression and prepare the nation for war. Until 1939, FDR's involvement in foreign policy had been sporadic. In 1936, he had been running for office when Germany invaded the Rhineland. In 1937, he had been in the midst of the court fight when Japan invaded China. In 1938, he was in the midst of the "Roosevelt recession" when Hitler invaded Austria. The September 1938 Czech crisis played out when FDR was still pursuing his November 1938 purge election. that ultimately failed.

Much less support had been forthcoming from progressive forces supportive of him when he needed to respond to the needs of possible war. FDR had been forced to seek support from a new grouping in the mixture of Republican internationalists and their Democratic allies in Congress. The Grand Alliance was successful only eventually by responding to the Japanese attack on Pearl Harbor. The country united against the foreign foe. The successful conclusion involved the large-scale organization of the latent power of American industrialization; gross national product doubled during the course of the war. However, the killing that occurred on the eastern front in Russia is what made the difference in defeating the Nazi German enemy. There were 300,000 dead among the Americans; there were 9 times as many Soviet citizens who died: 27 million. It was the most terrible in their history; for the people of the Soviet Union in 1945, their country was in a shattered state, lucky to have survived.

The Second World War was a victory over fascism only; not over authoritarianism. Moreover, the leadership of Stalin was undiminished; that of Harry Truman was inexperienced. Security for himself, for his regime and for his country and lastly for his ideology were Stalin's goals. Disproportionate losses during the war may have accorded the Soviet Russians with disproportionate gains but Stalin needed to have the accord of his former allies to achieve them. He wanted neither a cold nor a hot war. However, based on his Marxist-Leninist ideology, he predicted his eventual victory in Europe. He had indeed reached Berlin but recalled that Czar Alexander I had reached Paris after the Napoleonic Wars in 1814.

The history of the United States during the next fifty years was that of the "Cold War" with the development of Washington DC as the capital of the "free world" during what was indeed 'The American Century." Foreign policy took the major role aside from the intervals of the Johnson years around 1964; the government remained divided with the Republican presidency dominant throughout the years of the Cold War

Only during the First World War did the United States intervene in European politics. It claimed to make the world "safe for democracy," defined as liberal capitalism. Intent on withdrawing from direct intervention in Europe in favor of the United States, the country eventually intervened once again during the Second World War but then even more definitively and more lastingly. The accord among the Grand Alliance during the Second World War lasted until their victory. That accord, based on spheres of influence, began to founder. Suspicions arose colored by the actions of native Communist parties in France and Italy. The implementation of the Marshall Plan in Western Europe in 1947 and western moves toward the establishment of the West German state in June 1948 led to the formation of the Comecon in 1949 to organize ideological conformity on both sides of the Iron Curtain. The Warsaw Pact formalized the role of the Red Army in maintaining its coercive role established during 1945.

An American role toward withstanding what appeared to be active Soviet aggression in Western Europe led to the formation of NATO in April 1949. The key document for the American militarized response of the Cold War was NSC-68 created after the Soviet discovery of the Russian atomic bomb technology in the summer of 1949. The Korean War in June 1950 led the United States toward a global struggle with international communism. This also led to the production of the super H-bomb and the proliferation of nuclear war heads during the early 1950s. Although militarization had occurred, American organization for war was tempered by President Truman's avoidance of atomic war while American superiority remained.

French acceptance of German re-armament was conditioned by the integration of German iron and steel into the European Community starting in October 1954. The sense of the "Cold War" was maintained under the benign visage of President Eisenhower. Surrounded by the Dulles Brothers, he permitted the use of covert activities acting on nationalism as it continued to arise in Asia and Africa with its greatest potential for long-term consequences still acting in Iran. The fight initiated to support French colonialism in Viet Nam by John Foster Dulles led to the application of American forces in what turned out to be America's least successful war there. Coincident was the rising tide of civil rights that entered the very center of American political life during the Kennedy-Johnson Administration. The ongoing maintenance of the Viet Nam War for far too long during the Nixon Administration marked the persistence of the source of Richard Nixon's early career as a fervent anti-Communist.

Increased divergence from Soviet control in Eastern Europe and Germany occurred after the death of Joseph Stalin in 1952. The first revolt in East Germany in 1953 and then the subsequent revolts in Hungary and Poland in 1956 continued to illustrate the coercive role of the Red Army in maintaining Soviet control. Repression in Czechoslovakia had not gone well. Red Army officers had almost lost control of their troops when they had been jeered rather than welcomed, as they had been told they would be. The signing of a treaty between the two Communist super-powers in 1950 masked a degree of divergence first created displayed by the Chinese during the Korean War and further amplified by their independence of Soviet leadership.

This divergence became increasingly evident during the 1960's. It made possible for Richard Nixon to strengthen that divergence during 1972 as well as simultaneously abate the Cold War with the Soviets.

The defeat of the American forces in Viet Nam reinforced the Soviet form of social revolution under its auspices. The origins of the detente pursued by the Nixon-Kissinger team failed to deter the Vietnamese yet assured the Soviets that the militarization followed by the United States would be blunted without the threat of nuclear war. The SALT Treaties assured a degree of arms control while the Soviets could proceed with their local wars under the auspices of their local communist parties.

Watergate signified that might did not always make right. Americans placed law above might; Nixon had made several mistakes that were characteristic of him. The leaking of the Pentagon papers to the *New York Times* was not of such great significance. They were not comparable to the secession crisis that faced Abraham Lincoln in 1861 when he abrogated civil liberties. His second mistake was to employ such clumsy agents. His third mistake was to attempt to cover it up. The presidency had become encased in secrecy and subterfuge. The resolution of the Cold War would depend not only on the nuclear stalemate, but on the inability of the two systems to provide an adequate level of living as well. The great surge of world prosperity under American auspices was also coming to an end. There was also the rule of law - at least the basic standards of human decency should govern the actions of states.

This policy had been violated by NSC-68. Covert operations had been countenanced and encouraged in the name of "Cold War" morality. "Truth, honor, justice, liberty for all - the problem is how to preserve them...when we are opposed by people who scorn ...these values" wrote President Eisenhower in 1954. And so, the Cold War transformed American leaders into Machiavellians, acting according to necessity. Their resulting silence postponed from Eisenhower's through Nixon's tried publically to justify "not learning to be good." Rumors of American involvement in Iran and in Guatemala became so obvious that the CIA achieved recognition for what it did not want.

In Latin America, the Castro Brothers and Che Guevara vowed publically to translate Cuba into a Marxist-Leninist state. When they took power, the CIA failed to overthrow them and failed again to dislodge them. By 1979, the first Islamist state came to power in Iran. Instead of de-escalating, the Viet Nam War continued to escalate under Johnson; and then under Nixon. As the Cold War wore on, in many instances, they went from regarding these compromises in covert behavior as regrettable to considering them as necessary, then normal, and then even desirable. A kind of moral anesthesia set in, leaving the stability of the Soviet-American relationship to be valued because the ultimate was too frightening to contemplate any alternative.

The Helsinki Declaration included a human rights declaration in its Final Act recognizing the final effects of the Second World War division of Europe. It also became a manifesto of freedom in the satellite countries and even in the Soviet Union. What was being advocated was the individual behavior apart from that required by the state. When one person cries out, "The Emperor is naked", when a

6

single person breaks the rules of the game, he exposes it to be but a game. In the course of the 1970's in response to the failure of the Viet Nam War, the limits of the militarized response were exposed and the withdrawal of American domestic support for that effort.

The key element of detente was the arms control agreements. The three pillars of the Cold War were leadership of the capitalist world, geopolitical containment of the Soviet Union, and the rollback and containment of international revolution. The pursuit of the last came at a cost to the others. The return of American militarism with the Reagan Administration exposed the limitation of the arms control agreements based on "Mutual Assured Destruction." President Reagan's meeting with Gorbachev and his readiness to end the Cold War brought it to an end.

What seemed to end the Cold War was the readiness to entertain the notion of "American Exceptionality." Ronald Reagan, in his naive way, seemed to believe in that sense of religiously based mission that had originated in the mind of Henry Luce in 1941. That had given rise to the sense of the uniqueness of America's mission to do good for others as well as for itself. .

It may then have found expression in a similarly missionary-based but highly flawed sense of American right to control the direction of power during the earlier Eisenhower years under the direction of the Dulles brothers.

The number of cabinet members had risen since the time of the 1940's from eleven to nineteen in reference to the more complex world the presidency faced in the late 1980;s. With the proliferation of governmental agencies, the number of government workers had risen from 1.4 million to 3 million during that same period. The great success was recaptured in the years of the 1980's when victory in the Cold War vis-a-vis the Soviet Union once more renewed the sense of power that had energized the America of 1945. However, it was a much more chastened and a far different place from the city that had claimed the title in that earlier time of the 1940's as the "capital of the free world."

CHAPTER 1
MOBILIZATION FOR WAR 1938-1945

Introduction

No incident did more to advance the cause of racial tolerance than the concert Marion Anderson gave on the steps of the Lincoln Memorial on Easter Sunday 1939. When the "Daughters of the American Revolution" (DAR) refused, on the "basis of local custom," to make Constitution Hall available for an integrated concert, Sol Hurok suggested an open-air concert on the steps of the Lincoln Memorial, with the former president bow recognized as "The Great Emancipator." The Secretary of the Interior signed on; FDR gave his approval. "Tell Oscar {Chapman, assistant secretary of the interior) to have her sing from the top of the Washington Monument if she wants to."

An integrated throng estimated at 75,000 stretched as far as one could see. When Miss Anderson lifted her voice to sing *America the Beautiful*, democracy was redeemed. "When I sang that day, I was singing for the entire nation." Six weeks later, she sang at the White House for the King and Queen of England. The city's two hundred thousand white government employees went back to work the next day; many had worked there since the days of President McKinley. They remained. Washington for whites as well as blacks remained a Southern town; Southern in manner, and Southern in culture.

Like most Americans, FDR concentrated during the 1930s on domestic affairs when most Americans were still "ill-housed, ill-clad, and ill-nourished." FDR had sought to change the Democratic Party into a permanent progressive force; its urban base in the North was however hobbled by its base in the South. It would be those same Southern Democrats who would provide the president bedrock support to resist aggression and prepare the nation for war.

Until 1939, FDR's involvement in foreign policy had been sporadic. In 1936, he had been running for office when Germany invaded the Rhineland. In 1937, he had been in the midst of the court fight when Japan invaded China. In 1938, he was in the midst of the "Roosevelt recession" when Hitler invaded Austria. The September 1938 Czech crisis played out when FDR was still pursuing his November 1938 "purge election." The Munich Agreement and the dismemberment of Czechoslovakia in September 1938 was the important mark. The Gallup poll indicated that 60% felt that the agreement would lead to war.

The Election of 1938

After the impasse created in the Court plan in the previous Congress, it appeared to many of the liberals in the Roosevelt Administration that the actions of the Congress were not consistent with the country. They were not consistent with the overwhelming support given Roosevelt in the presidential election of 1936. Emboldened by the victory of Claude Pepper in Florida in the Democratic primary over his conservative opponent, Harry Hopkins, and Harold Ickes led to make the Congress better reflect the Administration. FDR weighed in against the "copperheads," and campaigned actively against Walter George in Georgia and Cotton Ed Smith in South Carolina. His aides also campaigned against Millard Tydings in Maryland. In his campaign as the head of the whole nation rather than as a leader of his party, FDR tried to create a "liberal" bloc in support of his policies by his radio addresses but failed to unseat any of these men whose power lay in the local Democratic organizations.

Once thought to be going the way of the Federalists and the Whigs, the Republican Party picked up eighty-one seats in the House and eight in the Senate in 1938. A major new figure was Ohio Republican Robert A Taft. 1937 had been one *"annuls terrible"* for FDR. The court fight, the new 1937 recession and the threat of a one-party government all played a part in this stunning reversal. Both in Ohio and Pennsylvania, intra-party squabbles influenced Republican gains. Labor unrest including the sit-down strikes influenced losses in Michigan. Although the conservative press rushed to call it a Roosevelt defeat, the Republicans who were elected carried a "liberal" coloration. Rather than identify with Hoover, they traced descent from TR. For example,

Thomas E Dewey, the shining light of the Republican Party, generally omitted frontal attacks on the New Deal but rather focused on matters of improvements in procedures and in administration.

It looked unlikely that FDR would run for a third term and that his coat tails were no longer attractive as a source of control of the Congress. Patronage had also become less available. The New Deal was coming to a close and Congress moved aggressively to dismantle what it could. Farm subsidies did not suffer but the Federal Theater Project was closed down. Although the conservative coalition did not set the legislative agenda, it had the power to limit any of Roosevelt's domestic initiatives. Thereafter, the emphasis came more and more on issues of foreign policy. The election of 1938 forced the president to turn away from anti-big business philosophy. It served as a prelude to the truce FDR gained with the Republicans to gain enough votes for his foreign policy program necessary to prepare for the coming war.nich

Although FDR largely succeeded in persuading Chief Justice Hughes that the national regulation of the economy was within the scope of the constitutional powers of the Congress and the Executive, he lost the ability to subordinate the Court to them. Hughes prevailed on the issue of the independence of the Court and the role of the Court as the final arbiter of the Constitution. By trying and losing, FDR made what turned out to be the worst blunder of his presidency.

FDR had sought to change the Democratic Party into a permanent progressive force; its urban base in the North was however hobbled by its base in the South. It would be those same Southern Democrats who would provide the president bedrock support to resist aggression and prepare the nation for war. Until 1939, FDR's involvement in foreign policy had been sporadic. In 1936, he had been running for office when Germany invaded the Rhineland. In 1937, he had been in the midst of the court fight when Japan invaded China. In 1938, he was in the midst of the "Roosevelt recession" when Hitler invaded Austria. The September 1938 Czech crisis played out when FDR was still pursuing his November "1938 purge election."

Like most Americans, FDR concentrated during the 1930's on domestic affairs when most Americans were still "ill-housed, ill-clad, and ill-nourished." On Sunday, December 12, 1937, the *Panay* incident reflected a direct Japanese attack on a clearly marked American ship anchored on the Yangtze River, An amendment to a bill currently before Congress was just a few votes short of getting to the floor that would require a national referendum before going to war. A Gallup poll reflected that 73% of those polled agreed with the so-called "Ludlow Amendment." Support against it in the House came to FDR mainly from the South; least from the Midwest.

November saw *Kristellnacht* amidst universal condemnation but still only 5% in favor of changing quotas for immigration in light of the refugees. FDR was at the nadir of his popularity; weakened by his intervention in the 1938 election, Persistent unemployment, exacerbated by the recent mini-depression made it unlikely that Congress would act to modify national quotas. When Senator Wagner and Representative Edith Nourse Rogers co-sponsored bi-partisan legislation to admit 20,000 Jewish children, it was turned down. Anti-Semitism lurked very close to the surface.

FDR became consumed with defense and foreign policy. A new coalition formed on Capitol Hill to support him made up of Wall Street Republicans and Southern Democrats, There was a cabinet shake-up and General George C. Marshall was now Chief of Staff of the U.S. Army. Harry Hopkins played the role formerly assigned to Louis Howe and was now in the Cabinet as Secretary of Commerce. On March 15, 1939, Hitler marched into Prague, violating the basis for the Munich Agreement. Hitler pulled his last surprise before going to war. Molotov and Ribbentrop signed their non-aggression pact in August 1939 and the war was on. Once again, now a generation later, a European war would intervene to create a new political alliance in the United States.

The March on Washington

The segregation of blacks in government agencies set up by President Woodrow Wilson had been quietly set aside. Blacks were employed at higher levels and in higher numbers than previously. There was actually an unofficial "black caucus" of sub-cabinet posts that included men like Robert Weaver of the Federal Housing Authority. It was at a symbolic level that the greatest strides were taken; and that by Eleanor Roosevelt. When she rose to fetch a glass of water for Mary McLeod Bethune; when she placed her chair demonstratively between the black and white sides of an audience in Birmingham Alabama, history was made. When she resigned from the "Daughters of the American Revolution" (DAR) to protest their refusal to permit Miss Anderson to sing, shock waves were heard around the world.

Senator Wagner had introduced an anti-lynching bill every year since 1934. It was certain to create havoc in the New Deal coalition. In 1935, the threat of a Southern filibuster kept it off the floor. It was telling that that threat was heavily supported by Northern Democrats as well as the usual Southern Democrats. 1936 was an election year. When the 75th Congress convened in January 1937, Gallup polls showed that 70% of Americans favored its passage. In the House, a discharge petition brought it out of committee and the bill passed the House for the first time. Both Speaker Bankhead of Alabama and Majority Leaser Sam Rayburn of Texas voted against. In the Senate, the Judiciary Committee voted it out.

FDR stayed on the sidelines. He had told Walter White of the NAACP that he needed the Southerners to help him save America. "By reason of the seniority rule in Congress, Southerners can block every bill I ask Congress to pass." When the bill came before the Senate, for the next six weeks, the Senate was snarled in a filibuster. Twice Wagner moved for cloture; twice he was defeated. The rhetoric of "mongrelization" had begun to appear, not unexpectedly, in the discussion of Mississippi Senator John Rankin but also acquiescence "to such demands beyond lynching" of that erstwhile "New Dealer" such as South Carolina Senator John Brynes. When FDR was asked to comment, he failed to do so.

Two techniques were in use by which the anti-lynching bill was sidetracked by FDR and the Democratic Party. One was to reduce the actual level of racism by ignoring it. The "South" was reduced to just another part of the country, like the "Northwest." The "south" was considered to be more ordinary, excising the Jim Crow dimension, if merely as a poor region, that could be melded within a larger sectional mosaic. Focus on aspects of the south other than race by racial moderates could discuss other aspects without confronting racial realities. The South was also seen as relatively dependent on northern capitalists, its colonialist character could be emphasized without addressing its racial complexion. The average wage for southern farm workers was in the range of 10 cents a day when the recent Wage and Hours Act had established something like twenty-five cents per hour for others. That act conveniently excluded black farm and domestic workers with additional provision for regional differences.

Education and health were similarly deplorable. The great majority of housing in the South lacked any system of sanitation. All these data lumped both whites and blacks without distinction. Organized white supremacy was the foundation of every aspect of southern environmental policies, economics, and society. Labor, in the form of the sit-down strikes and the labor unions of the Congress of Industrial Organizations (CIO) became the new factor in the Democratic Party that conveniently excluded the mainly black farm and domestic workers.

It was in the context of the concert at the Lincoln Memorial by Miss Anderson that A. Philip Randolph conceived the idea of a "Negro March On Washington" in 1941. As head of the entirely black "Brotherhood of Sleeping Car Porters," he had just successfully contracted with the Pullman Company, then the operator of railroad sleeping cars. Not merely an issue of unionization, it became a source of racial pride. Randolph was connected with the entire existing black political network including NAACP.

With mobilization for war in 1940-1941, employment had increased but not for blacks. Every branch of the military discriminated against or, in the case of the Marine Corps, excluded blacks entirely. The organizing group met with FDR without concrete results. Indeed the Democratic Party in the Congress and the ruling Democratic coalition was heavily dependent on Southerners. In frustration, Randolph began to organize what he initially hoped would be 10,000 marchers for jobs. It was couched in terms of the Government's concern for "economic security," a feature of the New Deal that differed from the previous ethos of "pioneer and rugged individualist" that prevailed in the case of the Bonus Marchers of 1932. What was also new was the demonstration that blacks could organize themselves and in large number without the need for whites and thus possible Communist taint.

The March enlisted widespread support from a coalition of black organizations ranging from the NAACP and Urban League to the Elks and black churches. However, some were concerned that the approach had become confrontational and unlike the quiet lobbying efforts of the past by individual black leaders. The route would go down

Pennsylvania Avenue past the White House to end at the Lincoln Memorial. Exposure of the thin nature of American Democracy would embarrass the United States internationally and at a crucial time in mobilization for war in the spring of 1941. Fearful of arousing racial unrest, in return for cancellation, FDR in June 1941 issued a highly significant Executive Order to remain in force until the expiration of his war powers. It forbade discrimination in Federal defense jobs. It also established a "Committee on Fair Employment Practices" (FEPR) to which one could appeal, the first such break via federal intervention. Segregation in the military was not addressed.

Mobilization for War

On September 1, 1939, FDR recapitulated his feeling in 1914 when war had been first declared a generation ago. In seeking repeal of the Neutrality Acts 0f 1937, Senator Borah spoke strongly on a nationwide hook-up; Charles Lindbergh did as well. It had originally been passed by an overwhelming 63-6 margin and represented a large constituency. "Isolationists" included those who admired Hitler who were members of the German-American Bund on the streets of Yorkville in New York, Communists who suddenly took a 180-degree turn on orders from Moscow after the Russo-German Pact, and Irish-Americans still unable to forgive Britain for its treatment of the Irish. A "cash-and carry" principle was voted as a stopgap for the belligerents. Bishop Sheil of Chicago and Al Smith of New York spoke, both designed to overcome Irish Catholic opposition to aid Britain. The Southerners voted for repeal as did several Republicans; western progressives and populists against. Stalin acted on his partition with Hitler of Poland and the war was on.

In the spring of 1940, as he took up his role as Prime Minister, Churchill already saw that the only place for the British to turn was America. Their ambassador Lord Lothian worked all though 1940 for the "destroyer for bases" deal that FDR, probably illegally, thought up to help the British in their hour of need. In December 1940, FDR, still hamstrung by the cash-an-carry provision of the Neutrality Acts, hit upon "lend-lease" as a means of providing war material with eventual payment left open. In his fireside chat dealing with the concept of the "arsenal of democracy," FDR used an example drawn from a work-day metaphor of "lending a neighbor a garden hose to deal with a fire" to illustrate the concept of lend-lease. Lord Halifax, the new British ambassador, succeeded in helping to create a shift in American opinion that turned Britain into America's revered ally, America's "special relation."

There was nobody in the offing who had the foreign policy credentials that were necessary. "Don't change horses in mid-stream" was the motto that carried the election of November 1940 and the third term shibboleth fell for the first time in the context of the German invasion of Western Europe and the Fall of France in June 1940. By March 1941, the U.S. Congress had appropriated $37 billion for defense, more than 4 times the entire budget in 1939. The size of the U.S. Army rose from 188,000 at the end of 1939 to 1.5 million by mid 1941.

Every step FDR took toward war was opposed. "The Committee to Defend America First" met to hear Senator Burton Wheeler of Montana and Senator Arthur Capper of Kansas oppose the war. In 1940, Congress had renewed the draft for one year. In 1941 the renewal was again up. Sam Rayburn encouraged Secretary of State Hull to write a letter encouraging the renewal. Four months before Pearl Harbor, the U.S. Congress passed the bill 203-202 to keep the armed forces intact and the draft operational.

In the end, the preparations for war were more costly, more hurried and unused industrial capacity enormous enough to succeed almost in spite of itself, and had a great pool of men and women eager to work anywhere, anytime, doing anything. And because the U.S. Government could apply the philosophy of the U.S. Army, an enemy can be overcome rather than defeated; and that if masses of men and material are sent in, the probability is that sooner or later, somebody will do something right. The American economy was converting to war production with remarkable speed. Demand from the British, and later the Russians, were bringing war material and for consumer goods that the belligerent nations could no longer make brought factories working at half-speed back to full production.

The United States had a large pool of workers eager to work anywhere and any time. This included the large exodus of black rural workers leaving the South to work in the factories of the North. In 1940, some 77% of black Americans lived in the South; by 1950 only one in three. During the war, unionization was far easier due to a shortage of labor in both the textile and tobacco industries as well as the earlier steel industry. And because the U.S. Government could apply the philosophy of the U.S. Army, an enemy can be overcome rather than defeated; and that if masses of men and material are sent in, the probability is that sooner or later, somebody will do something right. The American economy was converting to war production with remarkable speed. Demand from the British, and later the Russians, were bringing war material and consumer goods the belligerent nations could no longer make bring factories working at half-speed back to full production.

New plants would have to be built; private industry was not able to build them. The "Defense Plants Corporation" built these plants, such as "Willow Run" near Detroit, leased them to the private corporations. They were then sold at bargain prices after the war. The Army and Navy were even less well prepared to deal with the ancient equipment left behind from previous wars that was now out-of-date. Not only was the equipment out of date, so were the officers. The cavalry was unaware of the experience of the Polish cavalry that had been swept aside by Hitler's tanks in about a week. The army loved its hors4es and did not want to do away with them. They also did so well in parades. On maneuvers in the Louisiana woods, the men were given no ammunition to kill rattlesnakes for their guns that were listed as of 1910, left over from the 1917 war. Reports from the American officers such as Captain Maxwell Taylor who had trained at the German and Japanese War Colleges during the interwar era were ignored.

After the war had already been going on in Europe for a year, Lewis Johnson had remained as Assistant Secretary of War while Harry Woodring, the former governor of Kansas had remained as Secretary of War. The latter was finally replaced by Henry Stimson. A stalwart Republican establishment figure, the latter had been President William Howard Taft's Secretary of War and President Herbert Hoover's Secretary of State. Stimson might keep the Republicans happy and also help in the 1940 election. Frank Knox, the publisher of the *Chicago Daily News* and Alf Landon's former running mate in 1936, became Navy Secretary. Both spoke up in favor of abandoning the cash and carry provision of the Neutrality Acts and in favor of a peacetime draft. FDR could then follow through. In July, 22 Republicans joined 182 Democrats to put the extension of the draft bill over by one vote.

One of the first war agencies in August 1939 to allocate war materiel was the "War Resources Board" (WRB) led by Edward R Stettinius of United States Steel and Walter Gifford of AT&T. Unhappy with its composition, FDR then set up in late November 1939 "The Office of Production Management" (OPM), headed by William Knudsen of General Motors and Sidney Hillman of the Amalgamated Clothing Workers of America. Hillman had been instrumental in founding the "Congress of Industrial Organizations" (CIO) and in the involvement of his union in the CIO-Political Action Committee. Buoyed by sit down strikes and the development of industrial unions under the auspices of the CIO and the impact of the 1935 Wagner Act, still another factor had begun to exert influence in the Democratic Party.

The membership of the CIO had grown to 3.7 million in September 1937; the "American Federation of Labor" (AF of L) had also grown to 3.8 million by 1939. Moreover, these more racially integrated organizations brought civil rights into the counsels of the Democratic Party for the first time while black voters in the North began to vote Democratic after 1936 under the New Deal.

Neither Knudsen nor Hillman worked well with each other nor got business and industry to cooperate. Like the "War Resources Board" before it and the "War Industries Board" (WIB) of the First World War, it could only ask the businessmen to take charge; thousands of dollar-a-year men came to Washington to do so at multiple new alphabet agencies. Missouri Senator Harry Truman set up a committee in early 1941 to look into waste and corruption in the award of contracts. Rather than disband the ineffective OPM, FDR established still another agency, "Supply, Priorities and Allocation Board" (SPAB) under Donald Nelson. Formerly a buyer for Sears Roebuck & Co, then the nation's largest, he became head of the successor agency "War Production Board" (WPB). Nelson tried to get the Army Supply Command and the Navy to work together and with businessmen. The army's plan to replace Nelson with Bernard Baruch was abruptly changed in February 1943. From then on, crowded, confused and mired in its own customs and prejudices, relying on slipshod improvisations, Washington struggled to transform itself into the capital of the free world.

The Grand Alliance

On June 21st, 1941, the war took a decisive turn with the German invasion of Russia. FDR and Churchill met off the coast of Newfoundland in August to write the "Atlantic Charter," delineating their limited war aims and establishing an easy intimacy. They agreed on a "Hitler, first" strategy.

Relations with the Japanese had been on a downward spiral for some time. Without the personal attention of FDR, it had been in the hands of the State Department. Although the Japanese code had been cracked, the armed forces assigned such a low priority to decoding the messages that it took several weeks to decode them. Rather than accept the Japanese as a legitimate imperial power in Asia, American policy, tinged by racism, was condescending. After the Japanese victory over the Russian fleet in the Russo-Japanese War in 1905, many Japanese felt that Theodore Roosevelt (TR) deprived them of the fruits of victory. Russia was not to pay an indemnity and their possessions in Manchuria were safeguarded. The so-called "Gentlemen's Agreement" of 1908 closed off Japanese immigration to the United States; in 1913, Japanese were forbidden to buy land in California. Moreover, in 1932, the United States refused to recognize Japanese occupation of Manchuria.

Until June 1940, the Sino-Japanese War was a purely local battle but the Japanese military government took heart from the weakness of the colonial powers to consider getting their oil from the Dutch East Indies and rubber from Malaysia. The American oil embargo threatened their supplies and that an alternative supply line was thought necessary. Tokyo joined with Germany and Italy in the Axis Powers alliance. The Russians in April 1941 provided the Japanese with the non-Aggression Pact they needed. Despite the provisions of the Axis Pac, the Japanese decision was to go south to capture the former colonial possessions as a way to avoid the Russians in the north.

With precedence to the Battle for the Atlantic, the decision was to let the Japanese proceed to occupy the bases held by the Vichy French in Indo-China. It was FDR's intention to avoid war by permitting oil exports to go on. This decision was not followed by those in the State Department who were primarily in charge. Efforts by the Japanese Foreign Minister to negotiate were not followed up. The issue was not where the Japanese would attack but where and when. The attack by the Japanese on Pearl Harbor on December 7th brought the Americans into war officially. Russia was to be supported. The Big Three were the Grand Alliance but the war started in the South Pacific and there was a two-front war and a united country in the Congress.

Churchill came immediately, spent several weeks at the White House, addressed the joint session of Congress and agreed on the joint command structure in each theater. A North African invasion was planned within the year 1942. This ARCADIA Conference was the first in a series of such secret conferences. Churchill met with Stalin who apparently approved the decision to land in North Africa. Once done in November 1942, the Casablanca Conference took place that attempted to deal with the "Free French" movement and General De Gaulle. The next decision was to land in Sicily preparatory to an invasion of the Italian mainland.

The Battle of the Atlantic continued. A breakthrough occurred in December 1942 when the German naval code was cracked. B-24 Liberator bombers were assigned to provide air cover for convoys; they sank forty-one U-Boats in May 1943. Faced with the destruction of his fleet, by the end of May German Grand Admiral Donitz recalled all U-Boats from the North Atlantic. In the next months, not a single ship of 3500 that crossed was lost. The Battle of the Atlantic was won. At the TRIDENT Conference between Churchill and Roosevelt in Washington in May 1943, the decision was made for a cross-channel invasion in May 1944. The invasion of Sicily ended in Messina at the end of July. Several days later, King Victor Emmanuel precipitated a coup to bring Italy out of the war and the fall of Mussolini.

Churchill and Roosevelt met in the QUADRANT Conference in Quebec City in August 1943. They dealt with the details of the Normandy landings and the overall command to go to an American. They also discussed the atomic bomb. Instigated by a letter from Albert Einstein in the fall of 1939, the commitment to make a bomb was effectively started in January 1942. The resources for the "Manhattan Project" were committed to being carried out by scientists in the United States rather than Britain, but by both, in light of possible air attack in the latter.

Roosevelt had not met with Stalin; they were to meet in December 1943 in Teheran. FDR was hopeful that he could strike up a personal relationship with his Russian counterpart. The discussion focused on Germany; its degree of dismemberment. The date of the agreement for the invasion of Normandy was confirmed and the agreement to avoid the diversion of a British "approach through the soft under bottom of Europe." Stalin ended the toasts on a festive occasion with a toast to "American lend-lease." FDR, in turn, responded by comparing the Grand Alliance to be "a rainbow of many colors....moving unitedly for the good of ourselves and the common good." They were united in their common military goads as their highest priority. FDR decided that the commander of the trans-Normandy invasion would be Dwight Eisenhower.

The problem of European Jewry caught up in the Nazi death camps was ever present. The War Department from Stimson to Marshall to Eisenhower were adamant to the position that winning the war would be the goal and any diversion would be inappropriate. Most of the Jews that surrounded FDR were German Jews who were concerned about the impact of East European Jews on their own position in the United States. Career Foreign Service officers, called the stories of death camps "fantastic." Finally confirmed in December 1942, a joint statement was offered by the Grand Alliance holding the Nazis liable for their campaign. Any efforts to help rescue children or refugees were thwarted by the State Department. In January 1944, FDR set up the "War Refugee Board" (WRB) that sent Raoul Wallenberg to Budapest to save Jews being shipped to Auschwitz from the largest Jewish community yet intact in Europe. No further action took place.

The Election of 1944

FDR looked amazingly well on his return from Teheran over Christmas and early January. In January 1944, talk began to rise about the election campaign of 1944. He was examined for the first time at Bethesda Naval Medical Center and found to be in "congestive heart failure." His personal physician refused to explain the situation to FDR. His blood pressure remained elevated although his cardiac symptoms improved.

Henry Wallace was deemed detrimental to the ticket. Unlike 1940, when FDR had insisted on Wallace, he no longer did so. The choice was that of the big city bosses and the Southern conservatives in the Democratic Party. Although ER and FDR refused to agree, to the practical politicians involved, they knew that they were picking a president when they choose Harry Truman "as "offend" no one and "acceptable" to almost all. This was clearly instead of the preference to James Byrnes of the southern conservatives vetoed by the CIO as well as Ed Flynn of the Bronx for his lapsed Catholicism.

FDR was back again at Quebec City in September 1944 at OCTAGON Conference where the Morgenthau Plan for Germany was discussed, FDR seemed to be vague about its implications. Like an old war-house called upon for the last time, FDR rallied for this, his last campaign. He addressed his health issue head own; it was forty degrees and raining heavily when he started his daylong tour in an open car of the four major New York boroughs.

After his inauguration for his fourth term, FDR started for Yalta in January 1945. There the issue was the removal of the Red Army from Eastern Europe where it was already ensconced. At the time of this ARGONAUT Conference the Russians were fifty miles from Berlin; the western Allies had recovered from the Battle of the Bulge and were poised on the Rhine. The issue of Poland was paramount, but the events were in the saddle. The Russians were already in Warsaw. FDR seemed in good shape; he had gotten Stalin to agree to Russian entry into the Pacific War against Japan.

He died on April 12, 1945, almost lasting the entire war. Without knowledge of foreign affairs, Truman accepted the surrender of Germany, He participated in the Potsdam Conference with Stalin and the British. He agreed to the use of the atomic bombs on Japan and accepted the surrender of the latter along with the signing of the United Nations Charter, all within the first six months of his presidency.

Senator Robert A Taft, one of FDR's bitterest opponents spoke for almost all. "He died a hero; he literally worked himself to his death in the service of the American people."

Figure 1 – Harry Truman

Harry Truman was born in 1884 on a farm in the rural part of Jackson County near Independence Missouri. His father was an ancestral Democrat. He never went to college; worked as a farmer and timekeeper on the railroad. He volunteered for active duty in the First World War and was promoted to captain in the Field Artillery. He led his unit in the Meuse-Argonne Campaign. After the war, he went into business in Kansas City, which failed in what he had always called the "Republican" Depression of 1922. Known to the nephew of Boss Prendergast of Kansas City, Truman was chosen to County Judge and then presiding judge. During his first term as senator starting in 1934, he served on the Interstate Committee investigating railroad rates. He also acquired a reputation for integrity and supported the "Public Utility Holding Act" in 1935 as a mark of his devotion to the New Deal. With strong support from the railway unions, he was-elected narrowly in 1940. During the war, he was chosen to head the Truman Committee. Based on his genuine populist rage, he had an excellent reputation for reducing waste and corruption in the defense industry. He was a successor who could also be a Southerner acceptable to blacks and to other senators.

Although much of the building for war was in temporary wooden buildings, deliberately designed to remain temporary, there are several buildings that remain from that mobilization period even prior to the onset of American entry into the Second World War.

National Airport was built on made land across the Potomac. It replaces on its new site an earlier airport called Hoover Field that required planes to compete with traffic on the adjoining roads. .The completion of the National Airport finally provided Washington with a portal of entry compatible with the air age. Like Union Station of the previous generation of rail travel, the selection of the site and the design of the airport for this new era of travel were determined by its relationship to the grand design of the Nation's capital.

FDR made the decision in 1938 to support the new airport at Gravelly Point on landfill from the Potomac River rather than expansion at the old site further north or at places more distant from the city center. To overcome legal difficulties, the financing was from the federal budget. The airport remained under direct federal control until much more recent times. More controversial was the President's participation in the design of the terminal building. He wished to make the appearance compatible with the classic architecture of the Nation's Capital with the design somehow reflective of George Washington's home of Mount Vernon just downstream. Its central façade and spreading wings drew on Mount Vernon's form. To Roosevelt also was credited the inclusion of the columned portico in accordance with that of the original 18th century model. In his speech at the laying of the cornerstone in 1940, FDR invoked the development of American airpower to counteract the threat posed by the growth of the use of military air power by Germany, Italy, and Japan. An air armada of American warplanes filled the air immediately after his speech.

The projection of American power in the world was even more clearly reflected in the expansion of the Departments previously housed in the State, War and Navy Building adjacent to the White House. Even before the start of the war in 1941, a new building was being constructed at 21st Street in Foggy Bottom for the War Department. Found inadequate before completion, it was later assigned to the Department of State. In the 1950s, an extension was added in recognition of the increased scope of American foreign affairs.

The very much enlarged War Department site also needed to be compatible with the grand design of the capital. The original plan was to build near the entrance to Arlington National Cemetery across the Potomac from the Lincoln Memorial. FDR agreed with the Commission on Fine Arts in finding that site objectionable. Having such a large building so close to the Memorial Bridge would spoil the plan of the National Capital. Recalling his error as Assistant Secretary of the Navy in allowing the erection of the temporary Munitions Buildings for the Navy along Constitution Avenue, still then in use, he approved the final site to be south of Arlington National Cemetery.

During the Jackson Administration, in 1836 following the rebuilding of the Long Bridge, an early development was platted to be "Jackson City," in honor of the president. It became the site for a race track at the time of the Civil War; then in the 1870s, a gambling resort. Around 1890, the reputable residents organized a "Good Citizens' League" successful in cleaning out what had become the "Monte Carlo of America." During the 1920s, the area of the former race track became Hoover Airport, named after the then Secretary of Commerce .responsible for overseeing the nascent aviation industry.

The new office building of the Pentagon, the largest in the world, has become the epitome of the military power that still now characterized Washington DC. It was the nerve center no longer merely of the country but of the world. It also marked the start of the decentralization of federal buildings outside the District of Columbia and great proliferation of development that occurred in Northern Virginia during the post-Second World War period.

Most emblematic of the price of war was the building in Bethesda in nearby Maryland of the first portion of the Bethesda Naval Hospital. FDR had maintained his interest in the Navy since his office as Assistant Secretary of the Navy. To him is attributed the selection of the site then way off on Rockville Pike and the design of the tall central tower with the two low wings. The design was in line with the State Capitol of Nebraska that he had noted on one of his campaign trips, and in the tradition of a "stripped down" Beaux-Arts tradition that characterized the 1930s

Exemplary of the role of the United States as the leader of the Grand Coalition that liberated Europe is monument north of Arlington National Cemetery commemorating the Liberation of

Netherlands. *The Netherlands Carillon and Tower* recalls the ringing of bells throughout the country announcing the liberation from the Germans in May 1945. Queen Juliana of the Netherlands first presented the bells to the people of the United States at the time of her state visit to Washington in 1952. During the Second World War, Juliana, the only child of the then Queen Wilhelmina, lived in exile with her children in Ottawa Canada. She succeeded her mother as Queen in 1948 just before accepting the independence of Indonesia, the former Dutch East Indies, and the jewel of their empire. Due to an infection with rubella during the pregnancy, one of her children was born with serious disabilities that led to Juliana's support for children with disabilities in the underdeveloped world.

This theme of international contribution to the landscape of Washington was continued even by former enemies. The monumental sculptures of horses exemplifying *The Arts of War* by Leo Friedlander are at the edge of the Lincoln Memorial Circle at the entrance to the Arlington Memorial Bridge. *Valor* is on the left and *Sacrifice* on the right; each a rider astride the steed. *The Arts of Peace* by James Earle Fraser are at the entrance to Rock Creek Parkway; on the left is *Music and Harvest* and on the right is *Aspiration and Literature.* They were all completed in 1951 cast in bronze and gilded by the Italian Government as a measure of goodwill.

Figure 2 – Winston Churchill

With one foot on American soil and one foot on the British soil of its embassy, Winston Churchill symbolizes his dual parentage and his honorary United States citizenship but primarily his close relationship with President Franklin Roosevelt during the Second World War. The English Speaking Union funded this statue in furtherance of the Anglo-American "special relationship" that was so crucial to victory.

The statue shows the British Prime Minister at his greatest time with his fingers in the "V" for "Victory" and his ever-present cigar. The sculptor William Mozart McVey was born in Boston in 1905 but grew up in Cleveland Ohio. After training at the Cleveland School of Art, he lived in Paris. On the faculty of the University of Texas and Cranbrook Academy in Michigan, he returned as a faculty member of the Cleveland Institute of Art for the major part of his career. His playfulness is illustrated by his animal sculptures elsewhere but also by his humanizing portrait of Churchill.

Figure 3 - FDR Memorial

Following his death in April 1945, acting on his stated wishes, President FDR's only memorial was a marble slab "the size of my desk" in front of the National Archives Building on Pennsylvania Avenue. Considered by many as the greatest American president during both the Great Depression and the Second World War and the only one elected for more than two terms, he remained relatively unheralded. Although designed in 1978 before the Viet Nam Veterans Memorial, the Roosevelt Memorial was completed only in 1997 during the Democratic Party presidency of William Jefferson Clinton.

The FDR Memorial lies along the Tidal Basin amidst the cherry trees in the sacred area between the Lincoln and Jefferson Memorials. A landscape rather than a structure, the Memorial is unique among Presidential Memorials in its extensive use of water and its use of four areas or rooms to denote his four terms in office, related also to the "Four Freedoms" mentioned in his speeches. There are four sequential spaces containing statues such as a "bread line" and other sculptural elements each separated by a stone "garden."

Illustrating the times in which he lived, it describes the early years of the crashing Depression with a single waterfall. Multiple stair drops describes the public works such as the Tennessee Valley Authority. Chaotic falls at varying angles denote the chaos of the Second World War, and a still pool his death. Only after some controversy, Roosevelt is shown using a wheelchair, never seen by the public during his time in office.

The landscape architect Lawrence Halprin was born in Brooklyn New York in 1916. He trained at Cornell and University of Wisconsin, where he came under the influence of Frank Lloyd Wright at Taliesin east and finally at the Harvard School of Design under Walter Gropius and Marcel Breuer. His classmates there included Philip Johnson and I.M. Pei. Living in San Francisco, he built fountains and landscapes that invited human participation.

Second World War Two Memorials

The Marine Corps War Memorial was completed in 1954 north of Arlington National Cemetery as the first of the war memorials commemorating the Second World War. It replicates the famous photo of the raising of the American flag at the summit of the extinct volcano of Mount Suribachi on Iwo Jima in February 1943. Iwo Jima was one of a series of Pacific islands hard-won from the Japanese leading to the conquest of Japan's Home Islands. The Felix W. de Weldon statue incorporates the real faces of the men who had participated along with the steel pole and an American flag that still flies. The base is inscribed with the names of the Marine Corps engagements since 1775 and the tribute by Fleet Admiral Nimitz to those who fought to conquer Iwo Jima "Uncommon Valor was a Common Virtue."

The definitive World War II Memorial on The National Mall was long delayed until completed in 2004. The enabling legislation, passed in 1993, entrusted the building to the American Battle Monuments Commission with the responsibility for raising the estimated $100 million necessary. On the former site of the Rainbow Pool, it lies at the eastern end of the Reflecting Pool between the Lincoln Memorial and the Washington Monument. Its position in the monumental center of American patriotism recognizes its central position in the history of the United States in the 20th century. Considered by some as "vainglorious," it is clearly grand in the tradition of earlier monuments albeit differing from the themes of more modern monuments to the Korean and Viet Nam Wars elsewhere on the Mall.

Figure 4 - WWII Memorial on the National Mall

The architect Frederick St Florian was born in 1932 in Graz Austria. He studied at the Graz Institute of Technology and Columbia University. A long-time member of the faculty of the Rhode Island School of Design, he claims professional descent from Mies van der Rohe and le Corbusier.

Around his design there fifty-six pillars, two triumphal arches, a gold-star memorial wall, two waterfalls, four pools, eight monumental fifty-eight bronze wreaths, and twenty-four panels featuring images of the war. The selection of the central site of the Rainbow Pool was made by J. Carter Brown, head of the Commission of Fine Arts, as needed to establish the war's precedence over that of the lesser wars such as that of Korea and Viet Nam.

To some degree, the memorials already designed to honor some of the salient military divisions of the First World War were called into service once again to honor those of the second. For example, the 1st Division Monument in President's Park, first raised in the presidency of Calvin Coolidge in 1924, was renewed again in 1957. At that time, an exedra was added to honor those 4500 men who died in the Second.

The 1st Division was redesignated as such in May 1942, landed in England in August, and took part in the amphibious assault on French North Africa on 8th November 1942. In continuous combat from January to May 1943, it helped secure Tunisia. In July 1943, it was part of General George Patton's force in the invasion of Sicily and fought at a high cost to capture its mountains. Returned to England, it was in the first wave on Omaha Beach on 6th June 1944 suffering 30% casualties. It participated in the breakthrough at St Lo and the drive across France capturing Aachen Germany in October 1944. After action in repelling the German attack in the Battle of the Bilge in the Ardennes Forest in December 1944, the 1st Division reached Czechoslovakia before the end of the war in May 1945. It suffered nearly 20,000 casualties while earning fifteen Medals of Honor.

The Second Division Memorial at Constitution Avenue and 18th Street was similarly reconstituted in 1962 by wings added to the west in honor of veterans in the Second World War and to the east of veterans of the Korean War. At its first dedication in 1936, President Franklin Roosevelt paid his respects to "the splendid achievements of the Second Division." Constituted in September 1917, the "Indian Head Division" contained a Marine Brigade along with several U.S. Army regiments. It was unique among army units in having several U.S. Marine officers serving as division commanders. Entering combat in France in the Battle of Belleau Wood in the spring of 1918 to prevent the German advance to Paris, it fought at Soissons before taking part in the final Battle of the Meuse-Argonne. There were approximately 22,000 casualties, half Marines. It took part in the occupation of Germany until its return to the States in 1924.

The Second Division was unusual in remaining intact as an organization during the interwar era. During the Second World War, it landed at Belfast and was stationed in England in preparation for the invasion of Normandy. After landing on Omaha Beach on June 8th, 1944, it participated in the St Lo breakthrough to capture Brest, the heavily defended U-boat base in western France. After helping to stop the German Ardennes offensive in December 1944, the Second division reached the Rhine in March 1945, captured Gottingen and Leipzig in April before reaching Pilsen in Czechoslovakia by V-E Day in May 1945. It was in training for the invasion of Japan when V-J Day occurred in August 1945.

The sculptor James Earle Fraser, born in Winona Minnesota in 1876, was one of the most active in Washington during the 1930s. Trained at the Art Institute of Chicago and L'Ecole des Beaux-Arts in Paris, he was heavily influenced at first by his mentor Augustus Saint Gaudens. He is most famous for his Buffalo head nickel (1913) and his doleful *End of the Trail in* 1915.

Figure 5 –U.S. Navy Memorial *Lone Sailor*

A fountain is surrounded by a neo-classical Doric semi-circle that leads to the 8th Street vista to the Doric Old Patent Office created with the development of the north side of Pennsylvania Avenue in the 1980's. There is a huge granite map of the planet Earth showing the predominance of its oceans. To the side is the solitary standing life-size *Lone Sailor* with his duffel bag representing all those who have served and will serve in the U.S. Navy. Along the sides are reliefs illustrating the great ships in the historical evolution of the Navy.

Figure 6 - U.S. Air Force memorial

Much belated until the George W. Bush administration was there an opportunity to recognize the activities of the U.S. Air Force. The Air Force reached its independent existence as a result of its widespread actions during the Second World War. Once part of the U.S. Army, it became recognized by the formation of the Secretary of the Air Force as a member of the Joint Chiefs under the Department of Defense in 1950. The Air Force became a significant actor during the early part of the Cold War with its "Strategic Air Command" (SAC), the major weapon for the delivery of nuclear bombs. The delivery of atomic weapons by the nuclear-powered Polaris submarine was still another weapon delivery system that supplemented SAC following the Eisenhower years.

The U.S. Air Force Memorial was further delayed when in the 1990s it was designed to be placed near the Netherlands Carillion but was felt therefore to intrude upon the U.S. Marines Corps Memorial. Subject to litigation by Congressional Marine Corps partisans, it was redesigned to be placed in Fort Myer adjacent to the Arlington

National Cemetery. There it stands with three stainless steel rods that bend with the air currents. The three strands form the pattern offered by the famed "bomb burst" contrails demonstrated by the U.S. Air Force aerial flying team.

CHAPTER 2
THE TRUMAN PRESIDENCY/
POST-WAR ERA 1945-1952

Introduction

During the summer of 1943, FDR had spoken of the future in a fireside chat; in the fall, he spoke of conversion to peacetime for the first time. Since his early visits to Warm Springs in the 1920s, FDR had noted the wide disparities in education dependent on their locale. He saw the returning veteran as a means of leveling the playing field- a way to incorporate federal aid to education that could be politically irresistible. The G.I. Bill would provide not only education but also unemployment insurance and a host of other benefits. It passed Congress led by John Rankin of Mississippi and Missouri Senator Bennett Clark unanimously in June 1944 in the wake of the euphoria over the D-Day landings. Before the war, less than 5% of the nation's school-age population attended college; in the peak year of 1947 more than 49% of those attending college were veterans. Of the fifteen million who were eligible, more than half took advantage of the schooling opportunities available. It propelled an entire generation on an ascending curve of achievement.

On the eve of his presidency, FDR then had faced a situation far different from that faced by Woodrow Wilson at the end of the First World War. Then liberal political democracy had been the wave of the future. On his accession to power in 1933, FDR faced a far different world. With the exception of Britain, Scandinavia, and France, interwar Europe had turned authoritarian. The battle in the Second World War had been at least in part a battle in which the United States had led as a bastion of a liberal parliamentary democracy that had solved its problems without destroying its character during the difficult interwar years.

By the time of the Atlantic Charter in June 1941, FDR and Churchill had set their war aims to be a lack of physical aggrandizement. On New Year's Day 1942, 26 nations, led by the United States, Great Britain, China, and Russia, pledged their agreement to a document, written initially by FDR, pledging cooperation in the defeat of the Axis Powers. The choice of the words "United Nations" was that of Roosevelt, rather than the term "Association." In 1944 at the Dumbarton Oaks Conference in Washington DC, representative of the United States, Britain, China and Russia had met to draft the first version of the United Nations Charter. Stalin had agreed to FDR's proposal at Yalta for the voting procedures at the United Nations Security Council, Each member would have one vote but all major decisions would require the unanimous decision of the permanent members.

The meeting would take place in San Francisco soon after. Molotov would represent Russia. Secretary of State Edward R Stettinius, would represent the United States and would be chair of the American delegation to the UN.

President Truman's appointees had many things in common, most importantly their view of the world. All had been touched by Woodrow Wilson's "make the world safe for democracy." By that was meant "liberal democracy." All were full of a sense of America's greatness; of its helping to win the Second World War. This was to be in the editor Henry Luce's terms "The American Century." Capitalism was part of the wave of the future, as was the wave of technology and development. They believed they knew how to deal with the Soviets. Required was a strong foreign policy, backed up by enough military power to convince possible enemies. The United States was willing to fight for peace and democracy. The specter of no more Munich's hung heavy; appeasement leads only to further aggression and ultimately to war.

Stalin had achieved his sphere of influence with friendly nations on his borders. Could he be acting on the crest of Marxist dynamic for world conquest; that Marxism would eventually triumph? This was possible in Finland and at first in Czechoslovakia; it was not possible in Poland where the Russo-German Pact had extinguished Polish independence in 1939; there was evidence that recognized Russia as a menace to world peace. For these men; they had mobilized for war and could mobilize again.

The fruit of the Korean War was to prove American interest would shift somewhat from developing Europe's commitment against Soviet aggrandizement through the Marshal Plan and the founding of "North Atlantic Treaty Organization" (NATO). The appointment of General Eisenhower as commander was merely the first step that would take many years. The Korean War would shift American interest to the defeat of Soviet aggrandizement everywhere. This was to be done, not within the designs of limited budgets, but based on military budgets with far lesser concern for their height. As the first step, the budget was doubled for military affairs from $15 to $30 billion. After the end of the Korean War, the United States did not demobilize. The nation would support a standing army and a large defense budget as fears of communism roiled the Free World. The dreams of 1945 of peace and prosperity would be pursued but by a militarized state. This was to be done with less concern for attacking social concerns.

Of greatest consequence, 1948 marked the commitment of American foreign policy to a bipartisan policy of containment of the Soviet Union for most of the century to follow. Despite the wishes of Ohio Senator Taft, the selection of Thomas E Dewey and later Dwight Eisenhower would signify the commitment of the Republican Party to an internationalist stance. President Truman's blend of anti-Communism and domestic liberalism would define the center of the Democratic Party. The Great Debate was started by former President Hoover in December 1950. In calling for a unilateral "Fortress America," Secretary of State Acheson called it a retreat; President Truman called it a return to isolation.

Harry Truman was successful in bringing the Korean War to a possible truce without the use of the atomic bomb, in maintaining the demobilization without a depression, in dealing with the development of the thrust of the federal government created by the New Deal, and in its organization to support both prosperity while developing the response of the United States as the bulwark of the "free world." He can be credited with developing the structure by which the Cold War was to be waged.

Demobilization

Demobilization occurred rapidly. By the time of the Japanese surrender in August 1945, there were 8 million men in the U.S. Army and 4.4 million in the U.S. Navy. By the end of that year, the total had fallen to 3.5 million; by the end of 1946 to just 1.5 million. There were twelve under strength divisions in Europe by the end of 1947. The budget had fallen from $87 billion to $13 billion by the end of 1947. Nylon would be in the stores by Christmas. The OSS, the forerunner of the CIA, was disbanded by late September. The United Nations Charter was signed on June 26 and ratified by the U.S. Senate on July 28 by a lop-sided 89-2 margin, 26 years after American participation in the League of Nations had been rejected by the U.S. Senate.

In February 1944, FDR had already appointed a "Contract Termination and a Training and Re-Employment Administration." The memory of the dire pre-war economy lingered; the memory of the poor 1938 economy remained. The initial thrust of the unions had begun to focus on wages, hours and living conditions rather than the issue of participation in the economy. In his first post-war State of the Union message, President Truman had asked for a full-scale liberal program. He had presented a full-scale economic program including increased unemployment compensation, a continuation of the Fair Employment Practices Committee now that war powers would no longer exist and an increase in the minimum wage. For those Republicans and conservative Democrats who had thought the New Deal had been dead and buried, it was more than they had bargained for. It was more than FDR had ever asked for. The conservative coalition in Congress come back together, The House Ways and Means Committee with fourteen Democrats and ten Republicans rejected as a first step any increase in unemployment compensation. Despite the actions of the Congress, President Truman also asked for more like National Health Insurance; and in the midst of the demobilization of the military, a year of universal military training.

As post-war policies took hold, Southern Congressional issues took charge as the number of Republicans rose in the elections of 1946 and throughout the post-war era. The federal government could no longer take as leading a role in large scale planning that might jeopardize the Southern region's segregated social order. They could accept fiscal policy by taxation and budgeting but not planning by direct intervention in labor markets. Unlike their gingerly earlier support, Southern congressmen also began to interfere in preventing the incursion of labor unions in southern industries. By the end of 1946, the former concern with demobilization causing unemployment was replaced with concern for inflation and interference with the regional low labor characteristics.

The Second World War caused significant change throughout the country, but more in the South than elsewhere. Migration occurred off the land; to the North and unionization followed with an increase in black voting rights in the North. Not only did unionization occur in the South, but one in four farm-workers left the land as mechanization occurred. Attempts to lure industry to the area had begun to succeed; war industries accelerated roads and brought a million new civilian jobs to the area. There were, however, fears that black war veterans might not "stay in their place." There were six lynchings within weeks of the close of the war in August 1945; the Ku-Klux Klan began a rally at Stone Mountain near Atlanta.

The wartime FEPC had functioned under the presidential war powers; it had expired. Far beyond even that, the new bill would go to involve all hiring. The new bill reached the Senate in January 1946. Cloture of their filibuster was unsuccessful and the bill died as had federal control over unemployment compensation including the very sensitive area of agricultural processing workers, an area of black employment.

The shift of responsibility for employment had been shifted from the Department of Labor to the less friendly states, more friendly to the local racial policies; the 1947 Taft-Hartley Act limited the scope of unions. The planning component had been an intrinsic role of the "National Recovery Administration" (NRA); it had been declared unconstitutional by the Supreme Court in 1935. The commitment to *democratic* planning was nevertheless still another question. In 1939, the Brookings Institution published an analysis of how "an extension of governmental power over economic life could come about..." The former "National Planning Board" (NPB) had been established in 1933 under the "Public Works Administration " (PWA) of the Department of the Interior under Harold Ickes. Toward the end of the decade, the "National Resources Planning Board" (NRBP) had aimed at economic efficiency and to achieve social values to make a more egalitarian nation. It had been assigned the task of post-war planning to achieve "greater freedom for the American people."

At the same time, the "Bureau of the Budget" (BOB) had been established to be co-determines to establish an instrument of fiscal policy. Originally founded in 1921, it had been founded by the Brookings to increase efficiency in government. Moved to the Executive Office of the President, over the next half-decade, the BOB had become much larger and by 1944, the NPLB had disappeared. The BOB used a national budget to create a low-inflation, high un-employment economy. Not merely an accounting arm, it became a vehicle for fiscal policy and management.

The election of 1942 had produced a larger Republican Congress; the Southern Democrats could exert their will since they made up more of the Democratic majority of 222-209. Planning went into eclipse. It had provided the inspiration of the "Sixty-Million Jobs" of the 1944 election. However, Mississippi Congressman Whittington brought forth in 1946 an Employment Act and the formation of the "Council of Economic Advisors" (CEA). Its "hands-off" character distinct from planning made it far less threatening to the law-wage character of Southern labor.

The Taft-Hartley Act in 1947 was passed over-riding President Truman's veto. It excluded independent contractors under the law; prevented closed shop that required union shop for hiring and in "right to work" states made it voluntary to use the union even after meeting union shop procedures. In all the Southern states "right to work" laws were in effect, bringing labor organization to a halt. The exclusion of farm workers was broadened to the extent wished by the Southern congressmen along with secondary boycotts by unions acting on strikes by other unionized workers. The Southerners had become the pivot around which this far-reaching anti-labor initiative was taken on against the determined opposition of a Democratic president.

The Fair Deal

It was during the 80th Congress between 1947-1948 that President Trumann emerged as his own person. One of the most far-reaching actions of the Truman presidency was issued in July 1948 on the eve of the Democratic National Convention. President Truman issued EO

9980 that created the "Fair Employment Board" that combat discrimination in the civil service. Even more dramatic, EO 9981 abolished discrimination in the armed services, although vitiated by the reluctance of Southern officers. By doing so, President Truman re-enforced the connection of the black vote to the national Democratic Party in the North.

Nevertheless, President Harry Truman was no FDR; his voice did not command. He did not look the statesman. Public approval dipped from 60% to 35%. He could count on no cooperation from a Congress, controlled by an opposition party. The Republicans were hungry for control after a long period of weakness. They no longer were in opposition to the vote-getting ability of FDR. The Democratic Party was threatened by a split on both the Right and Left. President Truman's foreign policy, tempered by James Brynes, expressed considerable toughness toward the Soviet Union. The previous New Deal tilt toward labor had been tempered by the need for what would be a labor party in Minnesota and Wisconsin. In New York, the American Labor Party led by Vito Marcantanio still suggested a basis for a third labor party.

However, a third labor-based party did not evolve. The spirit of the New Deal liberalism did not evolve along the lines of the commitment to state planning; the overt celebration of government and the open skepticism toward capitalism and its captains. The original fight against monopoly engendered during the early days of the century and adhered to only in part was clearly abandoned. It had been abandoned in the spirit of the First World War and then fully abandoned in the production orgy that had occurred during the Second.

Liberals who had fought for public control over corporate power now no longer saw the need for such. American corporations had become socially responsible. Instead of lamenting the failure to achieve the reforms considered essential, they praised the New Deal for having solved the problems of capitalism without having intruded the state too far into the economy. They cited the contribution to the creation of a welfare state. They credited the state with the creation of the fiscal policies as the best way to deal with fluctuations in the business cycle and create full employment, ultimately those of John Maynard Keyes.

Henry A. Wallace, once vice-president, appointed Secretary of Commerce, was still allied to the Democratic Party. He had been asked to resign after making a speech against the anti-Soviet trend of American foreign policy under Secretary of State Byrnes.

During the New Deal, Henry A. Wallace was the Secretary of Agriculture, especially interested in the principle of leveling out the agricultural surplus. The millions of individual farmers, when confronted by reduced demand and falling prices, could not collaboratively reduce output to maintain prices. Rather, each farmer increased output to maximize individual income that then perversely lowered prices further. Historically, the Department of Agriculture had tried to help farmers increase production. Scientists at land-grant colleges developed more fruitful strains of corn and wheat, more bug-resistant cotton, more prolific breeds of cows and hogs. Willfully inducing scarcity goes against the grain of habits evolved since time immemorial of those whose livelihood comes from the soil.

On the insistence of FDR, Wallace was selected as vice-president in 1940 as the most likely to carry on the New Deal domestic policies. However, by 1944, FDR no longer supported his candidacy. On the very eve of the 1944 Democratic Party Convention, Wallace was notified of FDR's support for another. With the onslaught of the big city bosses and the strong antipathy of the southerners, Wallace had been labeled a Communist. Mississippi Congressman John Rankin used the Communist shibboleth freely in the 1946 campaign. Both Republicans and Southern Democrats used it in association with their anti-union rhetoric.

Muffling their own intra-party conflict, the Republicans submerged their differences in the 1946 mid-term election. With President Truman held back from the 1946 election because of low approval ratings, FDR's taped speeches were broadcast instead. The results devastated the Democratic Party and President Truman's status as a party leader. The 1946 election brought forth a Republican Congress; the first since the time of the 1928 Hoover election.

Figure 7 – Henry A. Wallace

The Wallace family, long associated with the ownership and the editorial policy of Wallace's Farmer Magazine, represented the interests of the corn producers in the Farm Belt. His father Henry C. Wallace (1866-1924), a professor of dairy science at Iowa State, was one of the founders of the Iowa Farm Bureau and long-time president of the "Corn Belt Meat Producers Association" and Secretary of Agriculture under President Harding until his premature death.

The son, Henry Agard Wallace born in 1888 on the family farm in Adair County Iowa, also trained at Iowa State College in Ames. Associated with the family magazine in Des Moines from 1910, he was editor from 1924-1929. A scientist, he developed a hybrid high-yield corn and founded a corporation Hi-Bred Corn (later Pioneer Hi-Bred) to market these strains. His concrete concern with crop yields and agricultural prices was mixed with occasional mysticism. Deeply religious, he was imbued with the spirit of the prophets such as Micah and Amos; in the precepts of the Sermon on the Mount. He stated his belief "in God and in progressive capitalism."

The "Progressive Citizens of America" formed by December of 1946 while the "Americans for Democratic Action" (ADA) re-organized to form a stronger anti-Communist Left within the Democratic Party. Eleanor Roosevelt and the Liberal Party under David Dubinsky of the "Ladies Garment Workers" and Walter Reuther of the "United Auto Workers" (UAW) formed the bulwark of the ADA. The decision by President Truman to veto the Taft-Hartley Act also served to safeguard to the Democrats the labor unions of the CIO-PAC including the Amalgamated Clothing Workers under Sidney Hillman. Although Henry Wallace had originally been seen as gaining millions of votes from the Democratic vote, his actual vote in 1948 was far less affected by a consistent effort to brand him as Communist. This was coupled with the death of Jan Masaryk, the sole non-Communist in the Czech government. Also associated was the important Berlin airlift to maintain the Allied presence in Berlin. That spring also marked the foundation of Israel whose prompt recognition by President Truman also created support of a group of potential Henry Wallace supporters.

During his 1948 campaign, President Truman responded to the threat offered by the Progressive campaign. At the Philadelphia Convention and on his "whistle-stop" campaign, President Truman undertook a vigorous advocacy of his "Fair Deal" program. The presidential attack on "no-good-do-nothing-- Republican-controlled 80th Congress" also included the liberal faction's civil rights led by Minneapolis mayor Hubert Humphrey. The Convention adopted a strong commitment to an anti-lynching and anti-poll tax and pro-FEPRC re-enactment. This precipitated the immediate defection of a fourth party: The States Rights Dixiecrats, but also a clearer identification by black voters with the mainstream Democrats.

The Housing Act of 1948 was the only major policy proposal to become law and created federal aid to urban governments. Originally sponsored by New York Senator Wagner, it followed the Housing Act of 1937 that created the U.S. Housing Authority. The earlier law's implications were reduced by inadequate funding constrained by the real estate interests. The subsequent act suffered from the same provisions. Housing projects continued to respect existing segregated patterns.

Like FDR, President Truman had consistent support from the urban bosses as illustrated by their support for his housing policy that remained under their control. The ability of the urban voting machines had begun to disappear over the course of the Fair Deal. During the New Deal, the plurality remained as high as 2.2 million in the election of 1944. During Truman's presidency, it diminished from 1.5 in 1948 to one million in 1952, coincident with the move to the suburbs and the changes in patronage but also by the housing policy that encouraged a move to the suburbs. By the end of the Truman era, the number of primaries had also begun to increase but the big city bosses still held power amidst the complicated welter of methods by which nominees are chosen.

President Truman had gained in fourteen preferential primaries over 60% of the votes to win the nomination. He won by drawing together the wayward pieces of the Democratic coalition. The Southern vote still stuck with the Democratic Party but the cracks were showing. The union members, Jews and Irish Catholics were still strong but fewer than before. Moreover, the Democrats regained control of Congress.

The greatest achievement was winning with social welfare proposals, alienating the most reactionary southern whites with his civil rights proposals and voters on the left most hostile to his foreign policy. Harry Truman held to his populist roots; to that of William Jennings Bryan, to its reformist Woodrow Wilson while making the world safe for democracy. He held the Democratic Party as had FDR as he held it to its liberal centrist role while advancing it in civil rights for blacks now entering the Democratic fold. As his last gift, the Trumann Administration supported with an amicus curiae brief the battle for desegregation of the public schools that the Supreme Court decree would carry forward under Eisenhower.

Strikes were ongoing. In the year following the end of the war, more than five million workers went out on strike that lasted far longer than before. One could say that what was occurring was closest to a general strike in American history. The most important was the steel strike that occurred in January-February 1946, in which nearly 750,000 were on strike. This was followed by a coal strike called by John L. Lewis for 5 cents per ton of coal for the union's welfare fund. During the first year of his presidency, the resignation of Harold Ickes and the withdrawal of Ed Pauley as Assistant Secretary of the Navy seemed to confirm President Truman as overwhelmed by events that he could not control. He was taking each crisis as it appeared, trying to be judicious but having no long-range plans.

In February 1946, Stalin issued a statement that capitalism and communism were incompatible and that conflict was bound to occur. Civilian rebuilding was to take a second seat to the build-up of the military. Just a week after this, a spy ring was uncovered in Canada that was implicated in the passage of atomic secrets. In March, the famous speech, Winston Churchill had taken place in Fulton Missouri in which he had invoked the principle that Britain and the United States must unite in opposition to the Iron Curtain. His apparent acceptance of the views expressed seemed inappropriate. However, just two weeks earlier George Kennon had sent his "Long Telegram" to the State Department issuing the recommendation that Soviet imperialism was merely an extension of long-term Russian imperialism. What was being recommended was "containment," to respond by force to possible expansion but to depend primarily on political and economic pressures.

The Korean War

President Truman's appointees had many things in common, most importantly their view of the world. All had been touched by Woodrow Wilson's "make the world safe for democracy." All were full of America's greatness; of its helping to win the Second World War. The famous "Long Telegram" of George Kennon had laid out the conditions for peace. They believed they knew how to deal with the Soviets. There was clearly a need to recognize Russia as a menace to world peace. Required was a strong foreign policy, backed up by enough military power to convince possible enemies that the United States was willing to fight for peace and democracy. The specter of no more Munichs hung heavy; appeasement leads only to further aggression and ultimately to war. These men had mobilized for war and could mobilize again.

American interest would shift from developing European support against Soviet aggrandizement through the Marshal Plan and the founding of "North Atlantic Treaty Organization" (NATO), the latter by 1949. The appointment of General Eisenhower as commander was merely the first step that would take many years. In January 1950, there was a general review in NSC-68 of the military strategy to be followed in response to the existence of the communist menace now that the atomic bomb could no longer protect Western Europe.

Based on the Long Telegram of George Kennan, the sense was that we were dealing with an unchangeable system ruled by a group that would require a costly and sustained effort over time, although possibly amenable over time. He found the history of traditional Russian insecurity, tempered by tyranny and clothed by Marxism-Leninism to be the combination that explained what they were doing. The decision to proceed with the H-bomb in February 1950 was made on the advice of Paul Nitze, and despite that of George Kennan. The work of Klaus Fuchs as a Russian spy had provided the Russians with information that could lead them to the H-bomb.

Paul Nitze was George Kennan's successor at the State Department's Policy Planning Board. He was entrusted with the development of the review of the strategic plan that culminated in NSC-86. Unlike a preparatory paper that Kennan had done earlier, he had described Soviet communism would eventually collapse when its inability to meet consumer demands and the freedom in the West became evident. In 1950, more hard-line views left Kennon isolated.

The Second World War had killed twenty-five million Soviets and destroyed half its industry. Kennon had recognized a USSR driven by its defensiveness and insecurity amid the destructiveness from its latest invasion by foreigners. Nitze's paper saw it animated by a new fanatic faith, antithetical to our own, that seeks to impose its absolute authority over the rest of the world. They used a CIA report that the Soviet Union might accumulate some 200 nuclear bombs during the next four years. The CIA had also issued a "sensible judgment" that the Soviets were not likely to attack. This "judgment" was rescinded, under attack by military analysts. The CIA changed its recommendation of imminent nuclear attack to conform to the wishes of those analysts. President Truman started the program that would increase the U.S. nuclear arsenal to 20,000 thermonuclear bombs by 1960 and 32,000 by 1966.

What was recommended was the development of the National Security Council, the CIA and the entire paraphernalia of the Cold War as well as a first-strike capability to deal with an unexpected sneak attack. There was a deliberately exaggerated threat facing the country that became the basis for American foreign policy for more than two decades. However, the onset of the Korean War in the next few months seemed to confirm this analysis.

The separation of Korea into its two segments at the 38th parallel had occurred at the end of the Second World War. It had been merely a distinction to facilitate the surrender of the Japanese troops stationed there. It had coalesced into the two separate countries; one in the north under communist control and one in the south under the no less authoritarian Rhee. The recent victory of the Chinese Communists had brought Taiwan into wide consideration as part of the defensive perimeter of American military power. Korea had not yet been brought into such.

However, the invasion of South Korea on June 24th, 1950 required a response. The occupation of South Korea was seen as a threat to the American interests in Japan. General MacArthur had already acted to bring American military supplies into the picture. The absence of Russia on the Security Council permitted President Truman to initiate the response as one by the United Nations. This aspect provided some important parameters into the military situation.

The North Koreans reached the South Korean capital within 48 hours and Rhee and his government fled. American ground troops were soon deemed necessary. It appeared to President Truman that the red line needed to be established in Korea as an expression of world communism. The Korean War in the next few months would shift American interest to the defeat of communism everywhere. The military budget was first doubled from $15 to $30 billion. The dreams of 1945 of peace and prosperity would be pursued but by a militarized state. This was to be done with less concern for attacking social concerns.

The invasion was apparently not instigated by the Soviets but by the irredentist North Koreans. Word from Moscow that the Russians would not enter the conflict encouraged President Truman to permit General MacArthur to land American combat troops in South Korea on the morning of June 30th. The American troops were not at first successful and the North Koreans overran the ROK forces that ran before them.

The issue of Korea would hang over President Truman for the rest of his presidency. The issue for him was to avoid the creation of a Third World War by keeping the Russians out as well as the Chinese Communists. The latter was compromised by the actions of General MacArthur. The American forces available in Japan were under strength and forces were cannibalized. Major-General Dean, the commander of the 24th Division was captured in combat on July 21st. American troops were playing against time hoping to keep the North Koreans from occupying the entire peninsula. With additional troops, the Pusan perimeter, a small area in the southeastern corner, served as a beachhead from which to advance. President Truman also insured that troops from other UN members be involved in fact as well as in principle. It was after all a UN "police action." For the first time in American history, permission was not gained from the Congress, although members of Congress were consulted.

MacArthur was able to launch an amphibious campaign far up the peninsula at Inchon By his Inchon landing, MacArthur reversed the situation and South Korea was re-established. The North Koreans refused his bid for unconditional surrender. MacArthur was authorized to advance with strict precautions to avoid the Chinese border. He assured the President at the Wake Island Conference that the North Koreans were prepared to make peace and the likelihood of Chinese intervention was "very little."

MacArthur then carried out his invasion of North Korea and brought Rhee to the North Korean capital of Pyongyang. All seemed to be going well.

Around early October, Chinese sources communicated their concern about the invasion of North Korea. Against orders from Washington, MacArthur unleashed his forces to approach the Yalu River border of North Korea with China in an attempt to bring North Korea under his control. Again, without orders from Washington, MacArthur had ordered the Air Force to interdict Chinese troops from entering North Korea at the Yalu River. Once again, President Truman was forced to accede to MacArthur's entreaties in view of the pending 1950 elections that led to serious Democratic Party defections.

MacArthur persisted in his claim that he could still succeed in the conquest of North Korea despite the incursion of Chinese troops. However, on November 24th, as many as 200,000 Chinese soldiers entered the battle. By Christmas Day, after great losses, the American forces were back at the 38th parallel. Despite General Ridgeway's appointment to the head of the Eighth Army and eventual success, the failure to succeed in Korea had been predicated on MacArthur's estimate that the war should be fought by expanding it.

Questions arose as to the use of the atomic bomb. President Truman's words had inadvertently suggested that it was a military decision to be decided by MacArthur. This was clearly beyond the scope of the United Nations coalition. The British prime minister, Clement Atlee came to Washington and received the assurances that no atomic war was being contemplated. In an interview with *U.S. News and World Report*, MacArthur disputed his expectations that he had offered that the Chinese would not enter the war and blamed political pressures for his failure to prevent such. Much discussion occurred in favor of MacArthur among the Republicans in Congress.

Republican Senator Robert Taft in January 1951 made his speech looking for a clear withdrawal from commitments abroad without a congressional mandate. President Truman persisted in his commitment to European defense as part of an overall priority. On February 12, 1951, Minority Leader Joseph Martin gave a speech in which he invoked the use of the Nationalist troops on Taiwan. He sought a response from MacArthur that expressed the latter's wishes to enlarge the war. This was despite the expressed wishes of President Truman to contain the war to the maintenance of South Korea. Eventually, MacArthur was forced to resign but not without severe repercussions to the reputation of President Truman.

The Declaration of a National Emergency on December 18, 1950, re-activated a number of emergency powers, but not all. By 1951, there had been the creation of the "National Security Council" (NSC); the "Central Intelligence Agency" (CIA) and the Department of Defense (DOD). The Department of State had increased its staff from four thousand to 24,000 in 1950 and a workforce in Washington from one thousand to eight thousand. This National Security State had been formulated to deal with the United States being freedom's indispensable guardian.

United against the new emergency unlike that of the Depression or the Second World War, the fear induced by the loss of the atomic bomb monopoly and the secrecy associated with it pervaded all aspects of national life. Under the threat of being "soft on Communism." and the threat of Wisconsin Republican Senator McCarthy, the availability of "secret" designation for much of national life provided an all too convenient cover for much that did not require such a designation and for far too long. Speaking in Wheeling West Virginia in September 1950, Senator Joseph McCarthy's sensational allegations of some 200 secret Communists in the State Department placed the handling of the "fall of China" to such sympathizers. The invasion of South Korea in June 1950 served to define the outcomes of such subversion and the need for secrecy. For example, the budget and a number of employees of the CIA were classified and its buildings in Foggy Bottom adjacent to the State Department were first so classified until freely noted by tourist guides.

The Great Foreign Policy Debate/The Cold War Debate

During the Second World War itself, there had been a discussion among the Big Three of possible spheres of influence. The British under Churchill had been intent on maintaining Greece as part of their own sphere of influence while acceding to that of the Soviets in Romania. In late 1944, Churchill had his own meeting with Stalin when they were said to have identified their respective spheres of influence. The same appeared to be the case for the Soviets in Hungary and Bulgaria. The post-Second World War history of the United States and Russia had first dealt with the arrangements for free elections to take place in Poland following the Yalta meeting. Even before his death, FDR was already concerned with that arrangement. At the Potsdam Conference in July 1945, the agreement on Poland for such free elections was reaffirmed. However, during the next year, the Polish interim government awaiting such elections was gradually taken over by its Communist components. Finally, in February 1947, in a fixed election, the Communist government prevailed.

The Cold War can be defined as starting with the so-called "Truman Doctrine" whereby American aid was extended to Greece (and Turkey) in 1947-1948. The existing right-wing Monarchist Greek Government had been destroying any opposition. The victor in the previous civil war with the support of a British army, they were now acting with the effect of driving the opposition into the hills to function as part of new civil strife led by Communists. The accord had been made such that the British would control Greece and had been permitted to do so by the Russians, and any attempt to interfere in Eastern Europe had been likewise accorded to the Soviets

Rather than view the problem in Greece as one of internal politics between factions, it was viewed by the national security staff in Washington in the spring of 1947 as part of an instrument of Soviet Communist expansionism. The attack on the Greek government was seen as part of Russian aggrandizement dating from the time of the czars. The so-called "Greek Democratic Army," was supported by the Communist regimes in Albania, Bulgaria, and Yugoslavia. The last offered aid in return for areas of Slavic settlement within northern Greece.

In March 1947, Stalin still had not given any significant Soviet aid to the Greek rebels but Yugoslavia under Marshal Tito had done so. As British support for the Greek Army was to be withdrawn, it was the unanimous decision for the American government to proceed to do so in the spirit of lend-lease. With American aid, most of the money destined for reform of the existing Greek government was instead devoted to military aid. The rebel force, deprived of aid by the Yugoslavs, now having left the Soviet bloc, was defeated. The Greek Army defeated the rebels with the re-settlement of a large number of peasants. This became a pattern to be replicated in later less successful stages in the Cold War.

The 1948 election marked the beginning of the end of the relationship between the connection between the presidential and congressional elections. There was a departure in the issue of party loyalty that would widen further in the name of personality and advertising and television. The withdrawal of the Southern congressional Democrats from loyalty to their president while they retained their identity as Democrats in Congress. This belied their connection with the presidential election that depended on victory in the northern urban states. The congressional elections of 1948 and 1950 marked that transition when even the foreign policy initiatives, let alone the domestic policy initiatives of the national Democratic Party went unheard.

The election of 1948 made some clear statements: The New Deal was here to stay, and an active federal government would seek to direct national development. President Truman's "Fair Deal" did not achieve very much but set the pattern for the Democratic Party. The South had begun to peel away, although not to the extent that it proceeded to do so in the subsequent Congresses. The black vote became anchored in the Democratic camp.

Of greatest consequence, 1948 marked the commitment of American foreign policy to a bipartisan policy of containment of the Soviet Union for most of the period to follow. Despite Ohio's Senator Taft, the selection of Thomas E Dewey and later Dwight Eisenhower would signify the commitment of the Republican Party to an internationalist stance. Truman's blend of anti-Communism and domestic liberalism would define the center of the northern Democratic Party

The Great Debate was started by former President Hoover in December 1950. In calling for a "Fortress America," Secretary of State Acheson called it a retreat; President Truman called it a return to isolation. The improved situation in Korea achieved by General Ridgeway served to calm things down. In his budget message for 1951, President Truman asked for an increase in defense expenditures to $72 billion from $42 billion the year before on its way to $92 billion the next year of 1952. All other domestic programs were kept the same or less. So the Great Debate continued of bi-partisan international commitment as needed to respond to the approach demanded of 'being soft on Communism" throughout the remaining years of the Truman administration.

What was to be done to get NATO to support its organization? The United States paid 76% of the contribution in 1954; France under DeGaulle in 1959 asked for the withdrawal of NATO troops from French soil. Massachusetts Republican leader Joseph E. Martin espoused involvement of Chang Kai-Sheik's troops in Taiwan into the Korean War. MacArthur was fired. The Republicans used this as part of their campaign of being "soft on Communism." Despite a warm welcome in the canyons of New York City and a joint session of Congress, Douglas MacArthur faded into history. "Old Soldiers Never Die...They Just Fade Away."

Ohio Senator Taft was the Republican leader who dubbed it "Mr. Truman's War." Rise in prices, profits and wages pointed to inflation in the absence of controls. In 1950, with a Democratic majority Senate the new majority leader Arizona Senator Ernest McFarland and whip

Texan Senator Lyndon Johnson reflected a bias against support of much of the presidential program. Truman's pressure for increased taxes to fund the costs of the war was met with a slow response by the Republicans and recalcitrant Southern Democrats who ran the Congress. The American people were not prepared to extend the war into Manchuria or to remain permanently at war on the Asiatic mainland. Yet, President Truman adhered to his commitment to maintain the limits of war; to not engage in an atomic war. War has to become merely an instrument of policy in the Cold War. It has to become so, regardless of differences in culture, ideology, and personal morality, because its weapons were so powerful, the results would be annihilation.

The economy worked fairly well during the Korean War. Although federal controls dwindled, inflation remained more or less in check. One can imagine how much Captain Harry, the war veteran, was tempted to take direct action to solve the country's foreign policy problems. It was as president that he spoke to maintain his limits and retire beset with crises.

In both his domestic and foreign policies, the Truman Administration confirmed the centralization created by FDR, and the New Deal would continue. Washington DC would continue to follow the path made by the Second World War and the federal government despite demobilization.

The Legacy in Washington of the Truman Years

The CIA was transferred to what was then a secluded spot in Fairfax County with the rather too transparent roadside designation of the "Bureau of Public Roads" directing visitors to it. People working for "the Agency" were told to identify themselves, ultimately to the public knowledge of all, as working merely for "a government agency." This elaborate government loyalty apparatus did not preclude serious breaches of security by spies that eluded the entire system.

The area, known as "Langley," was the title of the original plantation of the Lee family that owned that land adjacent to McLean Virginia. The first Headquarters Building was designed by the Harrison Abramowitz firm noted for the United Nations Building in New York. 1.4 million square feet in area, its cornerstone was laid by President

Eisenhower in 1959. A second even larger building was designed in 1991. Its size was not a measure of its success but perhaps a measure of its unwieldiness.

The Korean War had taken place many years before. It became commemorated on the sacred precincts of the Mall. The Korean War Veterans Memorial was not completed until 1995. Unlike the Second World War, there was no clear end point but merely a truce with a continued presence along the 38th parallel. There were no welcoming parades as individual soldiers returned home in the 1950s. The "police action" to protect South Korea from its neighboring Communist North Korea that took over 50,000 American lives seemed to fade into obscurity, to be "a forgotten war." The dedication of the Viet Nam Veterans Memorial in 1982 renewed interest in recognizing the veterans of the earlier war.

Although there were several similarities including a dark wall on which there were faces of soldiers rather than names, there was clear need to provide some of the realism that the symbolic Viet Nam Wall had initially avoided. Bronze soldiers as though on a night patrol celebrate the infantryman, the simple soldier. Their number of nineteen (with their shadows on the wall) is symbolic of the thirty-eighth parallel that divided Korea. They form a triangle leading to a pool of water, as does the peninsula of Korea jutting into the sea. Unlike its neighbor, it did not need to bring about reconciliation. The Korean War did not divide the country. The United States fought as part of an international coalition under United Nations auspices. The Korean Veterans Memorial placed in a grove of trees in the shadow of the Lincoln Memorial and across the Reflecting Pool from the Viet Nam Veterans Memorial together create a sacred triangle of memorials in the west end of the Mall.

CHAPTER 3
THE EISENHOWER YEARS 1953-1961

Introduction

Figure 8 - Dwight David Eisenhower

General Eisenhower had had a relatively apolitical career. He had first considered the possibility of a presidential run sponsored by a forerunner of the ADA while the Democrats despaired of running President Truman in 1947. Truman ran and won in 1948 but was tired and beset by both the Republican anti-Communist crusade and the attractive face of the conquering hero of the Second World War. It had been a truism of American politics after each successful war to welcome home the conquering hero. It had been true in the Revolutionary War in the person of the great General Washington; in the War of 1812 for Andrew Jackson, the hero of New Orleans; for General Grant in 1868, and now for General Eisenhower.

Dwight Eisenhower (Ike) was born in 1890 the middle of six brothers that grew up in Abilene Kansas. His mother cried after seeing him embark in 1911 on a military career to which she was so opposed on religious grounds. He did well enough at West Point, married Mamie, daughter of a wealthy man and entered into an interwar army career. His military career was aided as a protégé of General Conner with a thorough grounding in the principles of Clausewitz. After participating alongside General MacArthur in the withdrawal of the Bonus Marchers from Washington, he followed him to the Philippines in 1935.

Summoned to Washington by Army Chief-of Staff General George Marshall immediately after the start of war in December 1941, the rest is the history of the Second World War. After the war, Ike was president of Columbia University, wrote his book on the *Crusade in Europe* and then became commander of the NATO forces in Europe. By 1952, a group of wealthy men had agreed to fund his campaign for president as the Republican candidate based on being "the most highly respected men in the world." The call to duty brought him to seek the nomination and the election,

Richard Nixon was his vice-president to appease the Republican anti-Communists. This time they really had a chance for victory whereas Republican Ohio Senator represented the "Old Guard." On his election, nothing loomed larger than the Korean War. It had been going on since June 1950 and looked unlikely of satisfactory solution, wanting the solution offered by former General MacArthur for far-reaching atomic war. He would end the interminable war in Korea and not threaten the domestic New Deal-Fair Deal. Eisenhower projected a supra-public image in both 1952 and 1956 against the altogether too wordy and reluctant Adlai Stevenson. For the first time in twenty-four years, the Republicans won both houses of Congress in 1952. The Democratic minority in Congress was led by two Southern moderates: Texan Representative Sam Rayburn and Senator Lyndon Johnson.

When Dwight Eisenhower was inaugurated, he spoke of the forces of good and evil are massed and armed against each other and opposed as rarely before in history. Freedom is pitted against slavery; lightness against the dark, never before had two brothers, siblings whose ideology was so similar, direct both the covert and overt sides of American diplomacy. There was no need to hash things out; just by a wink could these two men work things out between them. Eisenhower encouraged the development of the network of alliances consistent with the role of the Dulles Brothers while Wisconsin Senator Joseph McCarthy rampaged through the Congress.

President Eisenhower belatedly inveighed against the "military industrial complex" while insuring its success by his very existence at its head during his administration.

Much of the action regarding civil rights was fought out in the Senate in relation to the process initiated for school desegregation following the 1954 Brown decision. In light of the opposition in the South and the lack of follow-up by the reluctant Executive, the passage of the Civil Rights Act of 1957 was considered merely a step. It confirmed the ambition of Lyndon Johnson as the "Master of the Senate" and his potential for becoming a national rather than merely a sectional leader. Although reluctant to use action to implement the desegregation of public schools, by the end of his administration, Eisenhower did so. It was his example in placing federal troops at Central High School in Little Rock Arkansas that started the incremental process that was to culminate in the civil rights acts of the 1960s,

The Men Around Him

In accordance with his military background, Ike selected New Hampshire Republican Governor Sherman Adams to be his Chief-of-staff. President Eisenhower prided himself on "having a clear desk." The rest of the Eisenhower cabinet was standard white-bread Republican. They shared an orthodoxy that shared his past. They shared the orthodoxy of the Chamber of Commerce speeches. The best government is the least government; anything that interfered with the freedom of business to make profits is inherently evil; the balanced budget is the most vital element of sound government.

It was most appropriate that Secretary of Defense "Engine Charlie" Wilson was his connection with General Motors no less than a labor union leader would be the background for a Secretary of Labor Martin Durkin. Engine Charlie cut research and development of missiles because there had been duplication. Secretary of the Treasury George Humphrey, chairman of M.A. Hanna Steel Company from Cleveland, represented the commitment to thrift that any GOP administration represented. Attorney General Herbert Brownell was the cabinet member that Ike knew best. He had orchestrated the campaign that brought Eisenhower the presidential nomination against Senator Taft in the name of internationalism and carried forward the election.

John Foster Dulles would be Secretary of State if a Republican were elected in 1952. The two brothers would be able to carry out their joint plans under the auspices of President Eisenhower's benign visage. An arrogant lawyer, and a member of the establishment Sullivan & Cromwell law firm, Dulles was a nephew and grandson of former secretaries of state. He had served presidents from Wilson to Truman and had been the *eminence grise* in foreign affairs to New York Governor Thomas E Dewey during his two runs in 1944 and 1948 as the Republican nominee.

While at Princeton, Foster served as his grandfather's secretary at the Second Hague Peace Conference in 1907 and graduation from law school at George Washington in order to stay with his grandfather. He then spent a year at the Sorbonne studying with the Nobel prizewinner Henri Bergson. He eventually became a partner at the law firm of Sullivan & Cromwell. Part of the American delegation to the Versailles Peace Conference, he later had a particular involvement in the design and execution of the Dawes Plan in reducing German reparations. Now the managing partner of his important firm, he did not close its office in Nazi Germany until 1935 and only against his personal wishes. Finally forced to give up his interest in supporting Germany, he became re-invested in his religiosity as an active member of the Federal Council of Churches and a proponent of international cooperation.

Figure 9 - John Foster Dulles

John "Foster" Dulles was born in 1888 the eldest of five children with his younger brother Allen closest in age. Their father was a vigorous Presbyterian, the product of a missionary tradition. It all blended together in his belief that America's destiny was to raise up the benighted masses elsewhere. His maternal grandfather John Watson Foster was a newspaper publisher in Indiana active in Republican politics. Only a short period secretary of state in Harrison's second cabinet in 1893, it was during that same period that the United States arranged for the overthrow of the Hawaiian Queen and recognized the new republic preparatory to its annexation. After his retirement from office, Foster developed a major law firm in Washington intent on arrangements for American foreign investment. Their maternal "Uncle Bert" made both brothers his protégés, living in the grandfather's mansion near DuPont Circle in Washington.

From both a religious and business background, Foster became more involved in Republican politics with the unsuccessful candidacies of New York Governor Thomas Dewey. As a Republican internationalist, he accompanied Republican Michigan Senator Vandenberg to the San Francisco Conference on the formation of the United Nations. One of his most telling post-war relationships was with the publisher Henry Luce. Of a similar missionary Presbyterian background, both believed that Providence had ordained for America its unique role,

Luce had written in 1941 of "The American Century," America's unique role in fighting Communism in this the 20th century. Both saw Soviet Communism underlying the nationalism in Asia, Africa, and Latin America. Soviet Communism became seen as "a great political force intent on our destruction." With the Truman Doctrine, President Truman accepted the need to place the United States in the forefront of the "free world." It was a godly crusade that was being fought against what was a godless enemy. The election of 1952 was carried forward as a holy war against infidels; you were either with us or against us. The Reverend Edward Elson of the National Presbyterian Center signed Eisenhower up right after his election. He was the first president to date to express his own prayer at the inauguration.

The Cold War was ever-present in Eisenhower's foreign policy. After having dealt with Korea, it was Dulles who dealt with French Indo-China by separating north from south in dealing with the issue of supporting French colonial policy there. The French professional army decided to take an opportunity for battle against the Viet Minh at Dien Bien Phi. Surrounded, they finally were destroyed. Ike refused to send the French what they wanted in the way of more than the war material that they had already received in large quantity. He refused to commit American forces initially.

He also had a role at the Versailles Conference with a position on the Boundary Commission along with a mistress from the Sphinx brothel.

Allen was busy post-war protecting American oil interests in the Middle East and graduating as well from George Washington Law School in 1926. Based on his brother's support, he also joined the Sullivan & Cromwell firm. Both brothers operated on behalf of their big business clients and governments, operating on behalf of both without drawing clear lines as to their responsibilities during the 1930's. The "Office of Strategic Services" (OSS) under "Wild Bill" Donovan recruited Allen who once again found himself in Berne, now during the Second World War. He was credited with carrying out the negotiations, hidden from the Soviets, that took the Germans out of Italy, several days before the surrender of General von Jodl at Rheims.

Figure 10 – Allen Dulles

Allen Welch Dulles was the younger brother of Foster Dulles born in 1893. Their childhoods were similar but their characters quite different. "Allie" was interested in many women, studied only at the last minute but still did well enough. After graduation from Princeton, Allie went to India where he taught at Ewing Christian College and met the Nehru family. He returned to Washington where his "Uncle Bert" was secretary of state in place of William Jennings Bryan in President Wilson's cabinet. Stationed in Bern during the First World War, Dulles became a true spymaster.

In the post-war world, it appeared necessary to re-establish an intelligence agency and Allen Dulles signed on to "The Central Intelligence Agency" (CIA). After the departure of President Truman, the agency eventually achieved both intelligence gathering and a covert role that acted in what they deemed American interests. Almost immediately after its formation, it intervened in the 1948 Italian elections to assure a Christian Democratic Party victory. Allen Dulles once again signed on, but now was free to do his will as Deputy Director for Operations, and then Deputy Director to General Walter Bedell Smith. Allen was in the way of becoming Director of the CIA with the end of the Truman Administration regardless of the consequences of the election.

The Two Dulles Brothers

Never before had two men, siblings whose ideology was so similar, directed both the covert and overt sides of American diplomacy. There was no need to hash things out; just by a wink could these two men work things out between them.

It appeared that the Soviet leaders were actively plotting to overrun the world; that their victory would mean the end of civilization and meaningful life and that they should be resisted by any means, no matter how distasteful. Both brothers personified this world view. Both partook of missionary Christianity. They both arose from the Calvinist tenets that Christians are weapons in the hands of God and His glory demanded that the reprobate be compelled to submit to the hand of God. As descendants of their grandfather, they were also descendants of 19th century America. Their family history reflected the history of the great American expansion. Moreover, their own personal history was embroiled in international banking and business. For decades, they had been involved in protecting multinational business would be to the advantage of everyone.

For the brothers, the great success of 1953 was to be Iran. Shah Pahlavi of Iran had become in 1947 a client of Sullivan & Cromwell to embark on a grand construction project to be carried out by clients of their law firm. Mohammed Mossadegh had been born in 1882, to a privileged family. Coming from a Shiite religious background, he was from a background that embraced martyrdom. He hated what foreign domination had done to Iran; it had stolen its riches. After the end of the Second World War, Mossadegh had become the leader of the nationalists in Parliament denouncing the British ownership of the oil industry. He also opposed the contract negotiated by the Shah with the clients of Sullivan & Cromwell in 1950. Mossadegh had been elected prime minister and taken control of the British governmental owned Anglo-Iranian Oil Company, also clients of the Sullivan & Cromwell law firm. Having disrupted what they considered to be the basis of the oil industry, Mossadegh was marked as a rabble rouser.

The British played upon American prejudices. They explained that Mossadegh had to be removed because he would lead to a Soviet takeover by the Iranian Communists. Once Foster had persuaded Eisenhower to authorize it, Allen was ready to carry it out. Kermit Roosevelt, the son of TR, was to be the CIA leader on the spot. The implications of arranging the take over of a nationalist non-Communist regime had appeared to be relatively easy short term victory. Its long term effects have continued to agitate the Middle East well into the 21st century.

The implications of such a policy were expressed in sites elsewhere in the world. Jacobo Arbenz threatened the status of the United Fruit Company in Guatemala by issuing a land reform law. The Dulles brothers had been personally involved with United Fruit's interests in Guatemala for many years. Arbenz was next on their list. In 1954, after the fall of Dien Bien Phu, Foster tried to support the French in their failed efforts. The decision was to partition Viet Nam halfway at the 17th parallel analogous to that of Korea, and to determine its future by subsequent elections. The rest would be but a postponement into the history of the next administration.

Their choice for leadership in South Viet Nam was a Catholic Ngo Dien Diem sponsored by New York's Cardinal Spellman in a country overwhelmingly Buddhist. He was to be supported by a CIA operative previously successful in the Philippines. During the ensuing year, a million persons living in the north of the country were carried to the south. Catholics, they were to serve as a basis for the southern leadership to prosper. The founding of "Southeast Asia Treaty Organization" (SEATO) was to be analogous to NATO but did not turn out to be of support to the budding government of South Viet Nam. Indeed, by bringing Pakistan into SEATO, Dulles supported the militarization of Pakistan and aroused the enmity of India. In 1956, the

Dulles brothers arranged an election by which Ngo Dinh Diem was selected to form the country of South Viet Nam to be supported by the United States at ultimate great cost.

The long awaited Geneva Summit Conference in 1955 brought the Soviet Bulganin and Ike together; not much was accomplished but the world breathed more easily. In the context of his heart attack, Ike's decision coupled with the actions of Khrushchev, the Cold War extended to Latin America, Egypt, and Africa. The rise to power of General Nasser in Egypt had brought him closer to the Soviets. Dulles abruptly withdrew the American promise of support for the Aswan Dam. The Russians offered to do so and Nasser took over the canal.

The Suez Canal had been built in the 1860s by the French. It was a highly profitable investment held in large part by the British government and a mark of British imperialism. It had been their ink to India among other things. On the eve of the 1956 election, the British and French counter-attack on the Canal Zone awaited the success that the Israelis under Ariel Sharon had already achieved. Ike failed to support the British and marked the beginning of the end of the British and French Empires in Africa. Simultaneously, the Hungarian premier Imre Nagy led his Communist government to withdraw from the Warsaw Pact. In response, Russian troops invaded Hungary's capital and deposed the rebellious government. After all the talk of more than "containment," there was no support for anything more in light of nuclear parity.

The effect of the Suez Crisis had its mark not only on the fate of the European powers, It marked in some way the elite in the United States that had grown up as members of the "Eastern Establishment." Trained in places such as Groton and Yale, they had been raised in the spirit of Anglophilia. They had been imbued with the idea that the United States and Great Britain were natural allies. Perhaps not as able as they thought themselves to be, nor as disinterested as they thought themselves to be, their underpinnings were threatened. Harold MacMillan signaled the change by cabling to his to his old friend Dwight Eisenhower "Over to you."

No one else could win for the Republican Party in 1956. The decision to run for a second term was couched as a "call to duty." That Nixon to be his running mate was not decided until the last possible moment. The Eisenhower-Nixon ticket won but had to be responsive to Khrushchev's bullying tactics until the latter was deposed in the long downward slide that would end in the late 1980's but not without the "missile gap" and a series of further scares.

The Tide of Civil Rights

Under Chief Justice Fred Vinson, the Supreme Court had been confronted by a series of "graduate school" cases based on the doctrine of *Plessey vs Ferguson*. The "National Association for the Advancement of Colored People" (NAACP) had brought those cases requiring "separate but equal" facilities in fulfillment of racial segregation under the 14th Amendment. "Separate but equal" still survived. After Chief Justice Vinson's death in September 1953, Eisenhower appointed Earl Warren as Chief Justice.

In May 1954, Chief Justice Warren announced that it was the *unanimous* opinion of the Supreme Court that in the field of public education the doctrine of "separate but equal" has no place. Seeking the "middle way," as was his wont, Ike routinely deplored "foolish extremists," suggesting a moral equivalency between those who sought equality and those who denied it. In 1955, in *Brown II*, the Court offered the interpretation that the ruling might "occur with all deliberate speed." This meant in practice much deliberation and little speed.

For the remainder of the Eisenhower administration, civil rights both confounded and annoyed him. As a military man, he had functioned in an all-white army; he had his friends who came from an all-white "big business" background. Yet he recognized the value of the ruling as part of the Cold War strategy. The "Voice of America" broadcast the ruling throughout the world. Prior to the Republican Convention, once again the candidate in 1956, Eisenhower demurred from supporting the Supreme Court decision on segregation of schools. He insisted on saying that his administration merely "accepted," it.

Figure 11 - Lyndon Baines Johnson

Lyndon Baines Johnson (LBJ) was born in 1908 in Stonewall Texas in the west of Austin. He was the elder son of a Populist member of the Texas State Senate and went to the "poor boy's school" of Southwest State Teachers College in San Marco Texas. He came to Washington as the legislative aide to Congressman Richard Kleberg (of the East Texas King Ranch). He was then Director for the New Deal Texas Youth Administration before going to Congress in 1937 as a Democratic Congressman from his own area in West Texas.

At the 1956 election, as by the election of 1954, the Republican Party in Congress failed of a majority. Lyndon Johnson was the majority leader of the Senate and Sam Rayburn the Speaker of the House.

His relationship with FDR was beyond the usual, the former intervened on LBJ's behave to a degree that went beyond the political for a young congressman. From the beginning of his career, LBJ strove for national power, to rise to the Senate, even to be a president. In 1948, he was elected to the Senate as a protégé of the Speaker Sam

Rayburn. Elected by very small number of votes, he was known to have stolen his election as senator but was saved by his lawyer Abe Fortas Introducing himself as "Landslide Lyndon," he kept himself under control. He cultivated Georgia Senator Richard Russell, the leader of the Southern Conservative Coalition. To an extraordinary degree in the seniority-bound Senate, LBJ became Minority Leader in 1952 before becoming Majority Leader in 1954. There he remained for the next six years throughout the rest of the Eisenhower Administration in which he successively created a new role for that office.

Now, LBJ was finally in the Senate but would it be too slow for him as his experience in the House had been too slow. He was firmly convinced that, like his father, he too would die at age sixty. For his sponsor, Sam Rayburn who entered the House in 1912, Rayburn did not achieve his first chairmanship until 1930 and then not become Speaker until 1940. Comparing himself only to be called by the presidential figure of the initials like FDR, *LBJ* was physically large; he was famous for his size; for his large hands and for his piercing eyes. He wanted to dominate every room or he wouldn't play. He had to believe in what he was saying; if he believed in it. He would "rev up." until you believed it as well.

The power of the seniority rule was established in 1845 when seniority within the length of time in the Senate (modified in 1921 by the length of time in the committee) became a cardinal rule in use with the chair determined by the majority caucus. This rule placed the important chairmanship in the hands of the "party barons," the committee chairs during a Democratically controlled Congress in the hands of the members from the Southern states. These men were frequently out of contact with the more liberal overall party platform such as that of the 1948 Democratic Party platform.

The "filibuster" was a term coined to permit a senator speaking at length on any subject. A curb on the practice came about in 1917 in Rule 22 when a cloture vote could be passed to end debate if two-thirds of the senators present voted for it.

The threat of a motion to change the cloture rule in itself was subject to that rule. Even during those rare Congresses in the 20th century when the Democrats were not in power, the Conservative Coalition following the 1938 election had enough northern conservatives from safe Republican states to retain their seats. Southerners helped Republican conservatives by their votes, to defeat liberal economic legislation. They in turn without enough black voters to punish them could tacitly refrain while supporting Southern efforts to defeat civil rights legislation.

LBJ had as his mission to gain national power. Yet, he could only gain power in the Senate by gaining the support of that Southern contingent by adhering to their opposition to their civil rights mantra. That, in turn, would prevent him from gaining the truly national power of the presidency. Although the eleven Southern states represented a significant number of the total number of senators; the major northern states represented a much more significant number of the electoral votes for the presidency. They were as much as 40% of the total electoral votes needed for the presidency. It was an article of faith, known by all, that no Southerner could ever be elected president, and president is what LBJ wanted to be.

Respected for his intelligence and integrity, he was also well liked for his helpfulness to others for designing compromises. Dick Russell supported national defense by his power on the Armed Forces Committee for any senator interested in having a military base in his state, keeping the farmer on the land and the school-lunch program as a support for farmers. However, the cause for which he fought the hardest was that of his Southland. Unlike the racism of such as the Bilbo's of Mississippi, Senator Russell would also attack, for example, the same Anti-lynching bill. His attack was more philosophical, but in terms of the principles of state's rights and sacredness of private property. Their Southern way of life was eminently worth preserving. It depended on preserving segregation, for the benefit of both races. Lynchings had been nearly eliminated. Outside federal force would merely cause resistance and violate the very foundation of the Constitution and was possibly Communist-tinged.

Figure 12 – Richard Russell, Jr.

Young Russell was born in 1897 the eldest son of thirteen of a family that had fallen on hard times as a result of the Civil War. Those battles he relived almost daily were those of his own Fort Lee when he re-enacted Pickett's Charge on the last day at Gettysburg. After graduating from the University of Georgia and its Law School, he ran for the State Legislature to capture the ambition of his father for statewide office. In 1929, he was elected Governor at the tender age of thirty-two. He did not talk down to his farmer voters, he was a Russell of the Georgia Russell's. Running for the Senate, he was a member of the famed crop of 1932 when the turnover was so great that seniority rules were in abeyance. He was given the opportunity on the Appropriations Committee, to be chair of the highly significant Agricultural sub-committee when the agricultural budget was increasing enormously.

During the 1950's he was able to continue his leadership of the Southern Caucus as it came under increasing attack. LBJ studied Richard Russell as he had his previous mentors. Like Sam Rayburn, LBJ cultivated the lonely bachelor; brought him to dinner and called him "Master of the Senate." Not until the Wilson era was there a party caucus that began to designate their leaders, known as "caucus chairman." Baronial chairmen's leadership still constituted most of the leadership, unofficial as it was. In 1913, the Democrats elected the first "whip," after the "whipper-in" of the British fox hunt who is responsible for keeping the hounds from staying.

In 1920, Alabama Senator Oscar Underwood became the first "Democratic Leader" sitting at the front row center desk. However, one rule in the one thousand page *Senate Procedure* that refers to him. If more than one senator requests the floor, recognition would go to the Majority Leader, then the Minority Leader. Elected Democratic Leader in 1925, Arkansas Senator Joseph T. Robinson was Minority Leader until the Roosevelt Landslide of 1932. Although himself from a farming family, he was personally opposed to any bills to alleviate farmers during the Hoover presidency. He only allowed the Senate to pass bills during the Hundred Days of the early FDR presidency; they were bills that he himself, as a typical Southern conservative, disliked. He saw his role to follow the wishes of the Executive and had no independent role before his fatal heart attack in the midst of the "court-packing" bill debate in 1937.

The Leader was not actually one who led in any way. He was merely one senator subject to the fifteen chairmen. If a Democrat, he was subject to the chairmen who were in every case conservative or Southern or both. This was so for Kentucky Senator Alben Barkley under FDR and Truman and then Illinois Republican Senator Scott Lucas under President Truman when Barkley was Vice-President. As President Truman pressed for changes in the area of civil rights, Congress refused to pass these laws. Although Dick Russell was the real leader, he preferred someone else to take the "leadership" position. This is what LBJ asked Russell to give him. So it was done in 1950 that he was given the "whip" position that apparently no one else wanted after but two years in the Senate and the "majority" leadership position in the next Democratic Congress in 1952.

In addition to being skillful in vote counting, LBJ was active in scheduling the votes for senators interested when their relatively non-essential bills might come to the floor. In his active way, LBJ became more and more essential to the working of the Senate. The election of 1956 had re-elected Eisenhower in the wake of the Suez Canal and the Hungarian uprising. The Democrats still hung on in the Senate. LBJ would still be the Majority Leader by 49-47. LBJ was unable to win the Democratic nomination; he was a *southern* candidate. He felt he had to get the Senate pass a civil rights bill. The black vote in the North had fallen in 1956 over 1952. Violence was rising in the South. Georgia had voted a constitutional amendment to close its public schools. The payoff would be the Civil Rights Bill of 1957, the first since Reconstruction and to be attributed to LBJ.

In order to do so, he had to dissuade the Southern Caucus from turning to a filibuster to enable him to still pass a bill that could have some value to meet the needs of the civil rights supporters in the North. That he would insure that the bill, if passed, would only be a token bill acceptable to the South. The question remains unanswered whether the decision was being made based on the likelihood that that would allow LBJ, a Southerner, to ascend to the presidency. There is no evidence that the assumption was otherwise at that time and would have been attested to by Dick Russell. LBJ had not given any evidence that he would do otherwise.

The heart of the bill offered by the Republican Administration by Attorney General Herbert Brownell to allow the Department of Justice take the lead in a broad array of civil rights making segregation illegal in schools and in public places. Part IV, however, had also addressed the issue of voting rights. Part III required anyone indicted for violation of any part to be entitled to a jury trial. What indeed did a white man have to fear from a southern jury? Although overall desegregation seemed too dangerous to Dick Russell, would voting rights be so safeguarded to be permitted? Was it moreover not a "constitutional" right? So it was, that voting rights would be permitted, protected for southerners by trial by jury. To make that rather meaningless provision acceptable to Northern liberals was that trial by jury was not required for civil contempt cases; that such would be available was long sought by railroad and mine workers unions. The liberal Senator Church offered the proviso that opened formerly closed juries to potential black jurors. So it came to pass that a Civil Rights Act was passed in 1957 without recourse to filibuster and credited to the work of LBJ rather than the Republicans as had been their original intent. Although much weakened, both desegregation and the right to vote would be redeemed by President Lyndon Johnson under his later auspices.

The 1958 election increased the Democratic representation in the Congress. The "Sputnik" controversy became fodder for LBJ's own Preparedness Sub-committee. Although Sputnik was dramatic, its military significance was minimal. The U2 reconnaissance equipped Eisenhower with the knowledge he needed for his reassurances that nothing more was necessary in the way of increased defense spending. Ever the poker player, Ike had bluffed while taking the hard line.

In practice, the number of tactical weapons had multiplied during his presidency. During the eight years of his presidency, he had held back spending on unnecessary or wasteful spending. In his eight years as president, he had forced the military to justify its programs. In a March 1956 meeting at the White House, he complained bitterly that it took the Army fifty years to get rid of its horses.

Even more than usual, this was far more complex than merely saying no. By deliberately invoking the use of atomic weapons, he was the only leader, by his military experience, who had the experience to try. In constant 2015 dollars, the expenditure is calculated to be in the range of $250 billion/each year with a rise to $264 billion in 1959 as a result of Sputnik. In his address, just prior to departure from office, Ike pointed out the balance needed for the long haul of opposition to the issues the country faced over time. It has been referred to as his warning of the power of the armaments industry going forward.

The Legacy in Washington of the Eisenhower Years

Figure 13 - Hubert Humphrey building

During the course of the Reorganization Acts of 1953, the formation of the Department of Health, Education and Welfare

(DHEW) took place out of the welter of agencies. Its origins derive from the Public Health Service (PHS) from the Maritime Hospitals under President John Adams in 1796. In the post-Civil War era, the Department of Education was founded to encourage public education. In 1939, these agencies were formed into the Federal Security Agency (FSA). It gradually accreted health agencies in the 1950's such as the much expanded National Institutes of Health (NIH), the much expanded Food and Drug Administration (derived from the Pure Drug Act of 1905) from the Department of Agriculture. Its first administrator was Oveta Culp Hobby, the former head of the Women's Army Corps (WACS) during the Second World War.

The building called The Hubert Humphrey Building was later one of the fruits of the trend toward modernity in the 1970's along Independence Avenue by Marcel Breuer, one of the Bauhaus architects.

The "National Aeronautics and Space Agency" (NASA) was created as one result that became LBJ's later special concern as Vice-President. The NASA Headquarters Building is amongst the executive office buildings clustered along Independence Avenue.

Figure 14 - NASA building

CHAPTER 4
THE KENNEDY-JOHNSON YEARS 1960-1968

Introduction

The energy brought to the Cold War by the young aggressive President Kennedy in his inaugural address seemed to be misplaced. The arc of foreign relations and the Cold War reached their crest with the Cuban Missile Crisis. The road to an atomic war then seemed to recede. The problems laid aside by John Foster Dulles in Indo-China were there to blossom into the Viet Nam War that was to grow into the American tragedy of the Cold War.

JFK's ambiguity had not resolved by the time of his assassination but had bloomed with the use of military advisers. LBJ sent the first 100.000 troops to Viet Nam in July 1965. When Walter Rostow moved into McGeorge Bundy's office, the concept of bombing and escalation had been well-established. Johnson's worst fear was to bring in the Chinese and recapitulate the Korean War. The experience of the Korean War began to capture the imagination of the political leaders. The DMZ differed from that of Korea; there was no boundary. The Viet Cong from the north walked around the boundary though the neighboring countries. The US Naval forces could not control the area from the sea on the east coast alone. Moreover, the South Vietnamese government did not have the support of the countryside. They were seen as the remnants of French colonial rule.

The tide of Civil Rights was to surge to become a tsunami that would explode into the mainstream of American political life. Its force in the legislature and the counterforce in both the South and North have marked the history of the rest of the century. The conservative backlash that ensued continues to roil American politics for the next fifty years.

The impact of the 1963 assassination of President Kennedy has reverberated in American history The events of the mid-1960's produced a politics that sharply increased the scope of American politics while simultaneously increased the projection of American military power. Both were at the cost of undermining faith in government action and military power, Lyndon Johnson and Richard Nixon were the two political leaders of the decade that followed 1960. Yet both failed to understand the new country that came into existence after the murder of the man who had beaten them both for the presidency in 1960. LBJ understood the South and understood what the South might be. He had little instinctive feel for the rest of the country. Accustomed to rolling up legislative majorities in the Congress, he could not see how to bring about change in the cities of the North. He tried to reconcile what could not be reconciled. He tried to win the war without truly winning it; to satisfy neither those who wanted to win nor those who wanted to get out. Unlike FDR who could express the needs of a leader when people could believe in one, President Johnson could not in the more process-minded 1960s.

The Election of 1960

Young Richard Nixon had been the anchor of the benign President Eisenhower to the anti-Communist roots of the Republican Party.

The success of the Eisenhower "middle way" despite Wisconsin Senator Joseph McCarthy depredations during the first term tore Richard Nixon from his roots as the anti-Communist candidate of the Republican right wing. Now with the second Eisenhower term coming up in 1956, Eisenhower kept Nixon waiting but finally accepted him as his vice-president. The Republican Party did not win Congress even in 1956 although Eisenhower's coat-tails should have sufficed. After the 1958 mid-term elections, the Republican right was further depleted in Congress with the loss of such as John Bricker of Ohio and William Knowland of California, the former Minority Leader. While Eisenhower consistently failed to implement school segregation, he carried it forward in Little Rock on a very limited basis. Now in 1960 Nixon was once more running but now as Eisenhower's successor.

The Democrats would have to offer someone stronger than merely a member of the previously winning team. Moreover, Nixon stood alone in his Party's favor; he had been decided upon early in 1960 when finally accorded Eisenhower's reluctant favor. There was no drama in his campaign. In the absence of its previous leaders, Arizona Senator Barry Goldwater had been elected in 1952 as the darling of the Republican right while Nelson Rockefeller had been elected governor of New York. Nixon stood alone with the still unified Republican Party only to have Goldwater become more dominant in 1964.

The 1948 election had been President Truman's victory. He had managed to hold together the FDR coalition of the labor unions and ethnic voters. The oratory of Alben Barkley delivered at the Convention had help buoy up the old Coalition one more time. The Northern blacks had become energized for President Truman in light of his limited efforts at desegregation while the Dixiecrats broke away from the national Democratic Party.

The Democratic Party regained Congress but was as badly divided as the Republicans. The Party in Congress was mainly made up of the Democratic Southern caucus who permitted President Truman to seek his "Fair Deal" fruitlessly. In 1956, LBJ had emerged as the leader of the Democratic Party with the 1957 Civil Rights Act the pallid result as his evidence of his national role. Johnson had always felt that the racial issue had always held back the South on its poverty, poor education and ignorance. He hoped that the Civil Rights Act would enable the South to make a step toward alleviating their problems. It would indeed be a forerunner of what he passed in 1963 while the South further departed from the Democratic Party.

JFK had been running for president at least from 1956 when he graciously deferred to the selection of Kefauver as Adlai Stevenson's running mate. The 1960 campaign put an end to the reticent candidacy that JFK was clearly running. However, he had to get the support of the liberal wing of the Democratic Party whose doyenne was Eleanor Roosevelt. In an exchange of letters, JFK denied that his father was spending money to elect the first Catholic president, although it was clearly true. Other liberals also questioned JFK but he succeeded in garnering a number of northeastern liberals to support him under Arthur Schlesinger despite the reluctance of Adlai Stevenson

Figure 15 – John F. Kennedy

John F. Kennedy (JFK) was the eldest living son of Joseph Patrick Kennedy. The Kennedy family ran as a unit under the tutelage of their father who had created the fortune on which they ran and the ambition that animated them. That ambition had become embittered as young Joseph Kennedy, the second generation son of a local political boss, had met with disdain by upper class Protestant Bostonians. Excluded from a "final club" at Harvard and then from the Cohasset Country Club, he built his large family as their refuge isolated by their Catholicism. His fortune made on Wall Street and Hollywood during the booming 1920's, he sold the market short as the Depression deepened. He joined the Democratic Party of FDR to become head of the Security Exchange Commission and the Ambassador to the Court of St James in 1938. From then on, having prepared each of them with wealth and self-confidence, he lived for the political advancement of his sons.

Jack Kennedy, sicklier and less driven than his elder brother, now carried the family's hopes. Equipped with a heroic war record and aided by his maternal grandfather's political allies, he easily won when running for office in his grandfather's solidly Democratic old congressional district in 1946. However, John F. Kennedy differed from his antecedents. Not the corny backslapping Irish politician arising from the streets of Boston like both his grandfathers, he represented for the now largely but not entirely middle-class Irish the sort that reflected their own strivings for upward mobility.

During his three terms in Congress, reflecting the advice of his father, he was only a "bread-and-butter" liberal while representing what was overall a poor working class district. He supported, without taking on the liberal ideology, the needs of his constituents for extending Social Security and raising the minimum wage. His family constellation came together to win him a senatorial seat in 1952 against the proverbial Yankee aristocrat Henry Cabot Lodge Jr. Tutored by his father's wishes, JFK failed to censure Senator Joseph McCarthy but had acquired the mantle of scholarship by winning the Pulitzer Prize for his *Profiles in Courage* book.

By the 1950s, although strengthened by his family, John Kennedy had become a person in his own right. His irony, intelligence, and charm had arisen in the context of his position in the family striving to counter the role of the perfect elder brother. Now, without strong ideological convictions, he was the glamorous exciting political celebrity brought into people's homes by television. Moreover, he could use ideas from divergent views and surround himself with persons of intelligence and strong convictions. He was firm on defense and compassionate on domestic issues.

The 1952 race for Senator against Henry Cabot Lodge was key. It was won by his father's money, his mother and sisters' teas and his brother Bobby's management. The family team was formed that would carry him to the presidency. His marriage to Jacqueline Bouvier in 1953 was the society wedding of the year; it made him more acceptable as a politician on the national scene. It is said that the decision to marry was urged by Joseph Kennedy upon his reluctant son as necessary for his career. After a short honeymoon, he soon reverted to his bachelor interests. His Senate career was once again affected by his ill health, this time by recurrent surgery for his back problems, complicated by his treatment for adrenal insufficiency. The hiring of Theodore Sorensen as his administrative assistant was very helpful in assuring Kennedy wide acceptance in the liberal intellectual community he otherwise lacked but only mitigated slightly his failure to vote for the censure of Joseph McCarthy.

Profiles in Courage came out in 1956. It won the Pulitzer Prize and helped earn JFK the credentials of a serious student of government, interested in moral values rather than short-term success. Written ostensibly while ill in Florida with his back problems, it aroused considerable popular interest and served to expiate in liberal academic circles some of the controversy around JFK's failure to disown Joe McCarthy. It was widely assumed that Ted Sorensen was heavily involved in creating it. Eventually, he received acknowledgement as one of the researchers and author of much of the first draft although not final authorship. Not merely a speechwriter for the inaugural and other important addresses, Sorensen also had a much larger role as an advisor on both domestic and foreign affairs.

Sorensen was hired by the newly elected senator in January 1953 to be, in his father Joseph P. Kennedy's words, JFK's liberal voice. JFK called him "my intellectual blood bank." They travelled together almost constantly during the years leading up to the nomination and election of 1960. Sorensen became his closest advisor and top aide and then Special Assistant when in the White House. Sorensen also had been impressed by the Harrington book *The Other America* on the persistence of poverty and had encouraged Kennedy to press forward on the poverty issue in the forthcoming election in 1964. This too was not yet developed when the killing of President Kennedy intervened and it became the first major new initiative during the Johnson Succession.

Figure 16 – Ted Sorensen with JFK

Ted Sorensen was born in 1928 as the middle of five children in Lincoln Nebraska. His father Christian Abraham (named after the president), of Danish ancestry, was the eldest of ten in a poor farming family. He was for a time in the 1920s attorney-general of the state. His mother Anis Chaikin was of Russian-Jewish ancestry. They met when he defended her, a suffragist and editor, when being prosecuted for her pacifist views during the First World War. The mother suffered from manic-depressive illness starting in her forties. The family was Unitarian and Republican of the Senator Norris Progressive type. Indeed, young Ted was named for the great Progressive Bull Moose candidate. He was first in his class at the University of Nebraska and its Law School before coming to Washington.

Aided by his father's fortune and political connections and his brother Bobby's efforts, President Kennedy contested several primary elections during the 1960 primary campaigns. Despite the support engineered by his father of the old-time Catholic party bosses in the Bronx, Buffalo, and especially Chicago, young Kennedy had to prove he could win despite his youth and Catholicism. The Kennedy money made his campaigning in the primaries such as Wisconsin far easier than that of Hubert Humphrey, his poorly funded rival. The numerous

Kennedys multiplied his impact across the state. After Wisconsin, came heavily Protestant West Virginia where his family wealth again won the day.

In the general election, JFK ran less against Eisenhower, the popular elder statesman, than against Nixon who cast himself as the elder's more energetic successor. Kennedy thus ran against complacency. He would get things moving, but he looked energetic and even younger and more self-confident than Nixon. Television had begun to play its role in projecting youth, attractiveness, and charm rather than content. Of course, in the election debates, what was important was who was the winner. In the case of the Nixon-Kennedy debates, Kennedy was clearly the winner. Nixon looked tired; Kennedy looked rested. Nixon looked pasty; Kennedy looked tanned. Nixon looked unsteady on his feet; Kennedy stood ramrod straight. Television became the factor to be reckoned with in all ensuing campaigns when appearances like these mattered.

As Garry Wills observed "It's the old story. For one of your own to be elected, he has to go out of his way to prove he is "not just one of your own." Invented as the first Irish Brahmin, Kennedy suggested a means of reinvention and identification for millions of others, Starting with his election in 1960, Teddy White in *The Making of a President* had created a picture of the inevitability of the election despite its actual closeness. The debates between Kennedy and Nixon were touted as the evidence for Kennedy's superiority of intelligence, wit, and confidence worthy of a president. Perhaps his most influential legacy was the process by which he achieved the presidency. Kennedy's election established the pattern for future elections of a dependence on money and television. Large amounts of money would be necessary to run for the presidency; private wealth would be almost necessary to build the needed early organization and the television advertising before one could garner further contributions. Large amounts of the time of any candidate would be spent in gathering contributions. The dependence on television would require candidates to be selected based on mere appearance and content of their speeches to be reduced to sound bites rather than substance. He had set into motion what has become a pattern with its own momentum far beyond its earliest practitioner.

The extremely close 1960 election marked the continuing dominance of the Democratic Party based on the even shakier coalition formed by FDR. The 1960 election had the highest recorded participation of any in American political history. The difference was around 100,000 votes. In Congress, the Republicans gained two seats; twenty-two seats in the House. The total was sixty-four Democrats to thirty-six Republicans in the Senate; two-hundred sixty-one Democrats (one hundred and one Southern) to one-hundred and seventy-four Republicans in the House.

Lyndon Johnson was a crucial factor in retaining Texas and several of the Southern states for the Democrats. The extremely close 1960 election marked the continuing dominance of the Democratic Party based on the ever shakier coalition formed by FDR in 1932 of both the Solid South and the northern cities. LBJ was fighting the anti-Catholic vote but also the white supremacy vote. The black vote held on or the Democrats with over 70% in the large cities of the North; the lesser 60's in the South. Catholics voted for Kennedy in a big way in Michigan, New Jersey, and Minnesota.

Eisenhower's participation had been held back somewhat based on Mrs. Eisenhower's private plea to Nixon. The Republican vote in the South had indeed gone up. It had gone up significantly in the New South cities of Atlanta, Houston, and Birmingham and their suburbs. States rights as a Republican principle boded well for the Republican Party in the South as well as in the Northern suburbs. Television made it no longer necessary to carry out a "whistle stop" campaign as in 1948.

The Thousand Days

In addition to the razor-thin presidential election, JFK had to contend with a thinner Democratic Party majority than in the previous Congress. The Democratic Party lost twenty House seats, all of them outside the South. Reverse coattail effects were also evident in northern states that he won wherein JFK ran lower than the Democratic votes for senator. Yet the Democratic president was widely expected to carry out the 1960 Democratic Party platform, one of the most liberal in history. The loss of northern Democratic Party seats bode ill for his liberal program due to the strengthened power of the conservative coalition in the House. Crucial to the fate of his liberal agenda was the role of the southern controlled Rules Committee chaired by Virginian Howard Smith.

Howard Smith was the chair of the gatekeeper Rules Committee, particularly vigilant to block any legislation that contained an amendment offered by Adam Clayton Powell, the Harlem congressman. That amendment would prevent federal funds from being provided if discrimination were practiced. If there were passage of a bill by the House, the threat of a filibuster by the even more conservative Senate would be certain to ultimately to kill any such bill. During each new congressional session during the 1950s, a civil rights bill would laboriously wend its way through the House and occasionally pass but not be considered by the Senate. Finally, the 1957 Civil Rights Bill passed with much fanfare and was billed as the first since 1875, but was actually emasculated by the requirement for jury trials.

The 86ᵗʰ Congress elected in 1960 consisted of 263 Democrats in the House while the Senate had 64 Democrats. Sam Rayburn from Texas was Speaker and John McCormack from Massachusetts was majority leader. Charles Halleck from Indiana was minority leader. The House committees were heavily dominated by southern conservatives. In order to maintain intraparty unity to pass bills dealing with economic issues, JFK felt he had to be circumspect in his advocacy of civil rights. To prevent Smith and his committee from blocking Kennedy's legislative program, Speaker Rayburn determined to enlarge the Rules Committee and did so, thus stripping Smith of his veto over legislation. The longest serving Speaker in the history of the House, Rayburn died in November 1961. His successor was John McCormack from Massachusetts while Carl Albert was selected as majority leader from the district in Oklahoma that abutted the one in Texas that Rayburn had represented since 1913.

Kennedy was himself particularly knowledgeable in foreign policy based on his extensive travel and longtime interests. He brought aboard McGeorge Bundy, the youngest dean at Harvard as National Security Counselor; Walt Rostow, a Yale Ph.D., and Rhodes Scholar was his deputy. Robert McNamara from the Harvard Business School and devotee of quantitative methodology from RAND to be Secretary of Defense who promised to bend that department to his will. Secretary McNamara discovered that the United States had a seventeen-to-one preponderance over the Soviets and the missile gap did not exist that had been bruited about during the election campaign. They did force out the businessmen and lawyers who had peopled both Eisenhower and Truman Administrations. House Speaker Rayburn confided to his protégé Vice President Lyndon Johnson that "he may be right that they may be as intelligent as you say but I wish any one of them had run for sheriff at least once."

JFK's election also marked the novelty of not only Catholics but also Jews in high places; Abraham Ribicoff and Arthur Goldberg were one of the most prominent. The latter was also a representative of the newer more activist branch of the labor movement based on principles of social justice rather than wages and hours alone. Arthur Goldberg as Secretary of Labor was ideally suited for his role but was soon chosen for the Supreme Court.

JFK's brother Bobby had been his closest confidant. As a member of the National Security Council and its various offshoots, as a bearer of the President's flag, name, and purpose in foreign affairs and as a participant in every crisis, he gave advice and assistance in foreign affairs totally out of context for his official position as Attorney General. This was in addition to his work more purely under his purview in the area more appropriately under the purview of the Department of Justice, in the field of civil rights.

The Kennedys regarded peace too important to be left to professional diplomats, Dean Rusk fit his needs to be self-effacing. Douglas Dillon as secretary of the treasury assured the role of a liberal Republican in the Cabinet. Orville Freeman of Minnesota was secretary of agriculture and Stuart Udall of Arizona as secretary of the interior were both energetic. The last was crucial in lending the crucial patina of culture to the Kennedy Administration. A friend of Robert Frost, Udall had first invited him to his home in Washington and persisted in his cultivation.

President Kennedy was confronted by an almost constant barrage of crises. His ease of command, his intelligence, and his historical perspective were useful when confronted with the problem of "The Bay of Pigs" and then the subsequent Cuban missile crisis. Rather than follow the recommendations of his military advisors, he took a longer view that avoided war in the Cuban Missile Crisis. He also avoided the moralistic approach of John Foster Dulles and saw the threat of power rather than ideology ultimately emanating from the Soviet Union. Although initially unsuccessful in achieving any détente, Kennedy tried to de-emotionalize the Cold War rhetoric and eventually achieved the first treaty with the Russians in limiting atomic tests in the atmosphere. As a result of the Cuban Missile Crisis, the Soviets did indeed follow through on Nitze's prediction in 1950. Embarrassed by being forced to withdraw from Cuba, they began a massive program to build up their nuclear forces to achieve parity by the start of the Nixon Administration in 1969.

Coming off the Bay of Pigs, in mid-1961 JFK sent Walt Rostow and General Maxwell Taylor to Viet Nam to look at how to salvage the game there. Military troops were not sent in but only "advisors." In the aftermath of the Bay of Pigs fiasco, JFK was persuaded by Walt Rostow to re-invigorate the issue of Viet Nam. The division of Viet Nam had arisen out of the Geneva Conference with the capital of Communist North Viet Nam at Hanoi. The division at the 17th parallel was to be temporary but the projected election was denied by the leaders of South Viet Nam in 1956. With support by the United States, a civil war appeared certain. In 1960, the North Vietnamese organized the "National Liberation Front" (NLF) that questioned the long-term viability of the South Vietnmaese state centered in Saigon. The premise of taking up the French mission was colored by the notion that it was the sort of problem in the Third World that warranted American intervention.

In his famous inaugural address, Kennedy started by invoking the rise of a new generation to power; a generation forged in the crucible of the victorious Second World War; the junior officers who had fought that war that brought the United States to the pinnacle of power. They were men in their forties who shared the conviction that the world might yield to their efforts; that "there was nothing we, or America, could not do." Like Theodore Roosevelt (TR), much of his appeal derived from the sense of adventure, of being a war hero. Like TR, JFK had young children in the White House. Also like FDR, he used charm and skill in manipulating the media in his press conferences and interviews with reporters.

The Democratic Party remained the uneasy coalition of the New Deal: Southerners, big-city bosses, northern liberals and labor. The last had been weakened during the erosion of the Wagner Act by the managerial counterattacks starting in 1948 and by the scandals of union corruption. Labor was still an important part of the coalition. The narrow success of Kennedy's election could be attributed to its success in getting out the vote of union members.

The modern civil rights movement is conventionally defined by the start of the Montgomery bus boycott in December 1955. Rosa Parks, an official of the Alabama NAACP, refused to move to the rear of the bus as required under segregation custom and law. Martin Luther King Jr, (MLK) recently appointed Baptist pastor to a church in Montgomery Alabama led the boycott. A student at Morehouse College in Atlanta, MLK had received a doctorate in theology from Boston University. While there, he had come under the influence of Dr. Harold Thurman, an apostle of the Gandhian Non-Violent Movement. After over a year, the boycott achieved the desegregation of the buses. King formed the "Southern Christian Leadership Conference" (SCLC) to continue civil rights protests.

However, there was no further civil rights action until 1960. In February, four students from North Carolina A&T in Greensboro North Carolina sat-in at a segregated Woolworth lunch counter. The movement spread to Nashville where there were several black colleges and then elsewhere. Formed soon after, the members of the "Student Non Violent Coordinating Committee" (SNCC) by their egalitarianism and non-violence were also challenging their elders and the hierarchy of the black churches. The response to the civil rights movement was led by the Department of Justice under the direction of RFK, the president's brother, and closest political advisor.

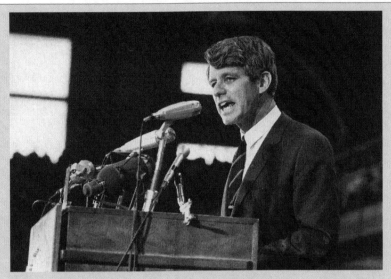

Figure 17 - Robert F Kennedy

Robert F Kennedy was the next but much younger of the Kennedy brothers. As the seventh of nine children, he was driven to compete. He attended many schools without achieving well in any; went to Harvard in the family tradition but, failing admission to the Law School, went to the University of Virginia Law School. More pious than his brothers, he sought racial equality, justice for the disenfranchised and compassion for the poor. His secular side identified with his father that showed his brash, rigid and hard characteristics. The latter aspect permanently tarred his reputation as the Assistant Counsel to the McCarthy Committee in the 1950s, a family friend. He later became the Majority Counsel when, after McCarthy's disgrace, the committee, now chaired by Arkansas Senator McClellan, embarked on its crusade against organized crime.

Starting in the senatorial campaign against Henry Cabot Lodge in the spring of 1952, Robert Kennedy found his role in his family and in his life as the campaign manager for his elder brother Jack. In the 1960 presidential primaries and then the presidential campaign it was Bobby that cracked the whip and played the dirty tricks that Jack could disavow. His appointment as Attorney General smacked of nepotism; it would put a man noted for his lack of diplomacy in the midst of a likely desegregation controversy. However, to his credit, the department came alive.

In the inaugural address of January 1961 by JFK that spurred Americans to a new activism, civil rights did not rate mention. Yet actions were being taken, on the very next day, James Meredith made his application to admission to the University of Mississippi. During the spring and summer of 1961 with the sponsorship of the "Congress of Racial Equality" (CORE), the mainly young inter-racial Freedom Riders confronted failure to implement the right granted by the Supreme Court since 1946 to integrate the interstate buses and the bus stations in the South.

When the "Freedom Riders" started in the spring of 1961, they had not yet aroused much popular support. The Department of Justice was primarily concerned about the risk of buses being burned. They were also concerned about the possibility of violence, of people being killed, but also of losing control. Litigation was the métier by which the federal government might enforce the actions of the Supreme Court leading to contempt of court citations; and in relatively rare instances and for relatively short periods, the use of armed force. The several hundred federal marshals were an interim force that could be deployed.

Despite the mobs who attacked them; and then the police who arrested them, more students continued to ride the buses. The pictures of burned buses spread throughout the world by television were detrimental to the image of the United States in its propaganda battle with the Soviet Union. Bobby Kennedy was also personally concerned how the situation might be embarrassing to the president meeting at that very time with Khrushchev in Vienna. RFK brokered an agreement to call off the rides in response to bringing the "Interstate Commerce Commission" (ICC) to act. Finally, in September 1961, the ICC acted to outlaw segregation in interstate transportation. What had been avoided for so many years and could have awaited additional years of legal delay was resolved rapidly on a moral direct action basis.

The next confrontation that came dramatically in front of the television cameras was the "interposition" of Governor Barnet of Mississippi in September 1962 to the entry of James Meredith to the University of Mississippi, the bastion of Mississippi racism. Meredith's entry had been prepared for long in advance. The federal marshals were there to escort him but the mob was far too large. The Mississippi

National Guard was federalized. The 101st Airborne was slow in coming but did come. The president gave a talk to the nation that night that incorrectly praised the university and the Mississippi authorities for their cooperation. The situation seemed to many a fiasco.

1963 was the 100th anniversary of the issuance of the Emancipation Proclamation. Yet the Civil Rights movement was stalled. MLK felt that there was a *coldness* in the response of the Kennedy's to the situation. Their goals were different. RFK saw the goal as a pragmatic political one to increase registration where it was indeed possible to accomplish it easily. MLK wanted to go to where no registration was possible to arouse the conscience of the nation and create a dramatic confrontation. The Department of Justice seemed unresponsive; they refused to intervene unless and until a bomb did actually go off not when there was a tip that a bomb would be planted. During this time, segregationist judges were still being appointed to federal judgeships in the South.

The comparison is made between FDR during the New Deal accepting that labor had to be dealt in order to preserve the structure of capitalism in the context of the sit-in strikes of 1937; so the blacks had to be dealt with while preserving the structure of white society. JFK had been reluctant to speak out on the subject of civil rights to any great degree while in search of the nomination, at the Democratic Convention and again in the Inaugural Address. JFK's concern about blacks was focused mainly on winning their votes. Indeed, his *Profiles in Courage* book had included the man whose vote prevented the impeachment of President Andrew Johnson. This was the man who had tried to forestall Reconstruction. In the Senate votes on the 1957 Civil Rights Act, JFK had voted for the jury trial provision that effectively gutted any implementation.

Given the loss of Democratic Party seats in the 1960 Congressional election, it appeared impossible, with the entire domestic program being held hostage, to gain any support for civil rights legislation. His public positions on civil rights had been, almost always, simply a reflection of his perception of its strategic value to him in pursuit of office.

Birmingham in Alabama was chosen by MLK to be the site in May 1963 for the beginning of what was called the "Children's Crusade" of young people marching for civil rights. They were met by Eugene

"Bull" Connor's men with their K-9 dogs and water hoses in full view of the world. Thousands were imprisoned but more came on successive days. 30,000 troops were encamped around the city and a thoroughgoing desegregation agreement was made in Birmingham, "the most segregated city in the South."

Shortly thereafter in June, George Wallace, the Alabama governor, carried out his threat "to stand in the schoolhouse door" to prevent the entry of two black students to the University of Alabama. This time, the troops were already nearby but it was merely a charade. No violence occurred; the students were quietly admitted escorted by Department of Justice officials and Governor Wallace withdrew. On the evening of June 11th, JFK made his famous speech invoking the full support of the federal government for desegregation as a moral crusade. He also planned to submit a civil rights bill to Congress in the teeth of the power of its control by the Southerners. That same night, Medgar Evers, the head of the NAACP and organizer of voter registration in Mississippi, was killed.

In August 1963, MLK made his speech at the Lincoln Memorial. Civil Rights had achieved national moral stature in the shadow of Abraham Lincoln. Although never carried out, the principle of the 1941 March on Washington had become more firmly established. Under the auspices of the Southern Christian Leadership Conference, Rev Martin Luther King Jr now spoke. It became the most remembered demonstration in the history of the United States. Under the auspices of the labor unions and a multiracial coalition of religious organizations, huge numbers came. For example, as many as 450 busloads arrived from New York City. Assembling on the hill around the Washington Monument, over 200,000 persons moved to the Lincoln Memorial. It was an aim of its organizers that the demonstration would be acceptable to the general public. It was part of what had been local actions throughout the South that had combined "the rhetoric of Christian expectations and American democracy with tactics of Gandhi's nonviolent direct action."

Figure 18 - Martin Luther King Jr. at the Lincoln Memorial

The use of the Lincoln Memorial for the 1963 March recognized the value of that site for the civil rights movement since the 1939 concert by Marian Anderson. The issue of reconciliation between the North and South was paramount when the Memorial was conceived and built. Before 1939 and even since, efforts by blacks were unsuccessful to modify that image by invoking Lincoln as Emancipator. Now, for the first time since Reconstruction, the principle of racial justice could find support by whites as well as blacks. The nationalism engendered by the Depression and Second World War could be united to the symbol of Lincoln to make civil rights for blacks part of being a true American.

Pulling together a coalition of white and black organizations once again as in 1941 were A. Philip Randolph and Bayard Rustin of the Brotherhood of Sleeping Car Porters. The latter, born in Pennsylvania, had strong Quaker roots. He had studied the elements of Gandhian non-violent resistance and contributed to the activities of the Freedom Riders who acted to test the public accommodation limits in the South. He had been an activist for a large number of causes throughout his life including the protection of the property of Japanese-Americans interned during the Second World War and helped found Conference on Racial Equality (CORE) based as it was on non-violent resistance. Imprisoned for his pacifist views during the Second World War, he was also a homosexual who often remained in the background of the civil rights movement to shield it from attack on that basis. Later in his life, he became identified with the Gay Liberation movement before his death in 1987.

Unlike the aborted 1941 March, the 1963 March had the cooperation of the president and invited the participation of white union and religious leaders. There was indeed a civil rights bill awaiting action in Congress. There was no note of civil disobedience. The success of this March in terms of numbers and the inspirational speech of Martin Luther King, Jr set the tone for many future protests. The Civil Rights Bill insuring equal accommodation was eventually passed under President Lyndon Johnson in June 1964.

The Lincoln Memorial and the statue of Lincoln have become fixed as an American icon representing freedom and equality in the spirit of Lincoln The Emancipator, the Lincoln of the Gettysburg Address and the Declaration of Independence. Even more recently, the statue of Martin Luther King across the road from the Lincoln Memorial captures that connection within the sacred precincts of American patriotism.

The trajectory of the civil rights movement had accelerated far beyond the wishes of the Kennedy Administration. It was met cautiously at first in the name of reiterating the "rule of law" but eventually had to be met more openly, particularly in light of the needs of the Cold War for America to represent human rights vis-a-vis the Soviet Union. JFK spoke in his June speech about "the events in Birmingham and elsewhere have so increased the cries for equality that no legislative body can *prudently* [emphasis added] choose to ignore…we face, therefore, a moral crisis as a country."

Figure 19 - Martin Luther King Jr. Memorial

There was a tacit admission that the Kennedy Administration would be influenced by demonstrations in the streets and Birmingham was indeed the deciding factor that led JFK to give his crucial speech and introduce the civil rights bill. JFK had begun to speak about it in moral, not merely legal terms, after placing troops in position to protect Meredith at Ole Miss, and now even more clearly after the confrontation with Governor Wallace at the University of Alabama that had been better handled. Introducing the bill was a step beyond what had been anticipated. His brother RFK had been alone in urging this action since the political support was not present in the Congress and the 1964 election was in the offing. RFK also was instrumental in making the March on Washington the inter-racial success that it turned out to be.

The bill passed the House Judiciary Committee with Republican support but was now under the jurisdiction of the House Rules Committee and its southern chair Howard Smith. There it stood on November 22, 1963.

The Kennedy Legacy in Washington DC

Although the time of the Kennedy Administration lasted but one thousand days, its legacy was far reaching and has had lasting importance in Washington. In laying out the streets and sites for the major public buildings in 1791 on the coastal plain between the rivers, Peter L'Enfant noted the existence of a "Ferry Road" that connected the Potomac River and its Eastern Branch. This was to be in large part the direction taken by his major east-west Street in Washington city to become Pennsylvania Avenue. He also recognized the natural eminences upon which to build with the connecting diagonals that would open vistas with "reciprocity of view." The most important was the eminence to the east that would form the platform for the "Congress House" (U.S. Capitol) connecting to the lower eminence to the west where would be placed the "Presidential Palace" (White House/ President's House).

The most central connecting the two important public buildings was given the name of Pennsylvania, central both to its site on the eastern seaboard and to the history of the country as the site of the previous capital city. Pennsylvania Avenue had precedence as the widest street; in a city of broad streets, its width at 160 feet connected the two major buildings representing the Legislature and the Executive approximately one mile apart. The distance between the two major public buildings seemed to defy its stated promise to be the great national Ceremonial Way. The early central business district arose on F and G Streets on the somewhat higher ground on a ridge to the north side of Pennsylvania Avenue. The area along the south marshy side clustered less desirable occupations. Not until the 1920s after the initiative of the McMillan Commission, the "Federal Triangle" replaces its earlier designation as "Murder Bay." Only then did the southern side of Pennsylvania Avenue reflect its significance for ceremonial processions.

Not until the 1970s, following the initiative of President Kennedy did the north side of the Avenue also begin to fulfill its expectation as America's "Main Street." The story is well known of the notice taken by the members of the 1960 Kennedy inaugural parade of the shabby nature of the North side of the Avenue. Initiated soon after was the "President's Advisory Council on Pennsylvania Avenue." The charge was to make the Avenue "lively, friendly and inviting" as well as dignified and symbolic. Its plan, presented to JFK on the very eve of his departure to Dallas, was then carried on by members of the successive administrations with major contribution and continuity provided by New York Democrat Senator Patrick Moynihan.

In 1972, the "Pennsylvania Avenue Development Corporation" (PADC) was founded to carry out the earlier mandate by bringing about cooperation between public and private sectors; to bring about the linkage between the Mall and the commercial and business part of the city. During the 1980s, much of the plan set forth in 1963 has been fulfilled with significant results that can be seen in the new vistas fulfilling many of L'Enfant's original ideas with particular impact on the new north side of the Ceremonial Mile.

One of the first fruits of the redevelopment of the north side of Pennsylvania Avenue was the plan for a large new building for the Department of Labor. It was not actually completed until the Carter presidency in the 1970s. Named after Secretary of Labor Frances Perkins during the New Deal, at 2nd Street and Constitution Avenue, it replaced the previous rather small Department of Labor Building in the Federal Triangle. That earlier neo-classical building adjoined the Mellon Departmental Auditorium by Arthur Brown, also the architect of the San Francisco Civic Center.

The Department of Labor was split off from the dual Department of Commerce and Labor in 1913 in the last hours of the Taft Administration to represent the interests of labor as an outgrowth of the progressive movement's concern with working conditions. It initially included the existing Bureaus of Labor Statistics, the Bureaus of Immigration and Naturalization and the Children's' Bureau. The Bureau of Immigration had its major concern with finding work for those immigrating. Its responsibilities for mediation and conciliation were a large part of its activities during the First World War. The first secretary was the secretary-treasurer of the "United Mine Workers" (UMW) clearly devoted to "the interests of the wage earner" that he established as the ongoing motif of the department. In eclipse during the 1920s, it gained far greater responsibilities during the New Deal under Secretary of Labor Frances Perkins to be recognized by its own building as part of the Federal Triangle however overshadowed by others in that building complex.

Following the original design of Peter L'Enfant, several other vistas were created. Looking north on 4th Street axis from the entrance to the East Gallery of the National Gallery of Art is the vista called John Marshall Park opened in 1983. The vista leads to the Old City Hall at Indiana Ave and F Street between 4th and 5th Streets N.W. Built in

1820, it rose on the knoll assigned by L'Enfant to the Judiciary. This building was a joint effort with the Federal Government since one wing was assigned to be a courthouse. The center portion served as the City Hall until 1873 when it was taken over by the Federal Government for use as courts. Its design was replicated in the subsequent adjoining court buildings built over the succeeding century.

This Greek Revival building with its Ionic portico is the only building remaining in the District that was the work of George Hadfield. A British-trained architect, he had been for a short time one of the series of architects involved in the U.S. Capitol in the late 1790s. He was said to be sponsored by Thomas Jefferson who, as a recent widower, had a brief relationship with Hadfield's sister Maria Cosway. Hadfield also was responsible for designing the earliest version of the Executive buildings adjoining the President's House for the Departments of State and Treasury. His work can also still be seen in the Arlington House, the Doric-pillared Custis-Lee Mansion overlooking Arlington National Cemetery.

The statue of John Marshall at the head of the vista is a copy of the one now in the Supreme Court Building. Born in 1755 in Fauquier County Virginia, John Marshall was the eldest of 15 children. His career moved through stages: the Virginia Assembly and Congress before becoming Chief Justice in 1801 remaining until 1835. Appointed by John Adams in the last days of his Federalist Administration, Marshall in his long tenure gave direction to the as yet uncharted character of the Judicial branch of the Constitution. He established the principle of judicial review and the role of the Federal government in relation to that of the states.

The area looking north from the National Archives on the 8th Street axis of Pennsylvania Avenue toward the Old Patent Office is now designated "Market Square" in recognition of its long-time use. One of the original lots reserved by George Washington for the use of the United States Government in 1797, Center Market in 1802 was identified as lying between 7th and 9th Streets south of Pennsylvania Avenue. It was called "Marsh Market" before it was called "Center Market." One could shot ducks in this marshy area. Tiber Creek flowed where Constitution Avenue now runs along the northern border of the Mall with the eastern portion of the Mall always a soggy place.

After a fire in 1870, the old Market House was replaced in 1872 by an extensive building designed by Adolph Cluss, the leading architect in Washington at that time as well as the architect of the Eastern Market at North Carolina Avenue on Capitol Hill. The center of the first streetcar lines, by the 1920s it was the largest retail market for fruits, vegetables and meat products. it was removed starting in 1928 in preparation for the building of the Federal Triangle.

The 8th street axis now looks to the vista of the Old Patent Office on a knoll originally designated by L'Enfant to house the equivalent of the Pantheon in Paris to honor famous Americans. Robert Mills, the architect of the Ionic-columned East Front of the U.S. Treasury was also responsible for at least the interior plan and structure of original South Wing of the Patent Office on F Street with its Doric columned portico, patterned after the Parthenon in Athens. Robert Mills was one of the first American-born professional architects. A protégé of Thomas Jefferson, Mills was one of the pioneers of fireproof construction with the use of concrete. He built Greek revival governmental buildings in many settings. Appointed by President Jackson in 1836, he was responsible for carrying out several of the new series of stone "public buildings" for the Executive Departments that would reinforce the image of Washington as a national capital.

He built the new fireproof building for the Patent Office, then a highly important Federal Government department. The building now contains, in the spirit of its original purpose suggested by L'Enfant, the "National Portrait Gallery" as well as the "Smithsonian Museum of American Art."

In 1967-1972, the massive brutalist style FBI Building dedicated to its long-time Director J. Edgar Hoover arose on the north side of Pennsylvania Avenue between 9th and 10th Streets opposite to the Department of Justice Building in the Federal Triangle. Although not "friendly or inviting;" to its credit, the FBI Building when it was built in the late 1960s was the first to adhere to the setbacks planned for the improvement of the north side of America's Main Street.

J. Edgar Hoover, after whom it was named, was born on Capitol Hill in Washington in the area of Eastern Market. He trained at George Washington University and remained one of their most honored alumni and a trustee until his death. He joined the Department of Justice during the First World War. Becoming head of the Enemy

Aliens Registration; he helped organize the raids led by Attorney General Palmer deporting radical aliens in 1919. He was appointed head of Bureau of Investigation in 1924 and of the "Federal Bureau of Investigation" (FBI) in 1935. Hoover became famous in pursuit of bank robbers during the 1930s. He directed the FBI to investigate possible subversion and civil rights organizations while the Mafia prospered during his time. In charge of counter intelligence, he used his power to collect possible incriminating information and remained an all-powerful Director of the FBI until his death in 1972.

Freedom Plaza is the major addition by the PADC to the north side of the Avenue. The Avenue here splits with a northern branch containing the former E Street bordering the National Theater and the new Marriott Hotel at the northeast corner of 14th Street. The remainder of the Avenue runs along the southern edge of the Freedom Plaza. The flat most easterly section contains a heroic equestrian statue of Casmir Pulaski clad in the cloak of a Polish Field Marshal. First gaining fame for his fight for Polish freedom against its partition by its neighbors, he volunteered to join the Continental Army in 1777. He died when wounded in the battle of Savannah in 1779.

To the west is a raised map of Washington as originally designed by L'Enfant. Across 14th Street is a wooded area called Pershing Park. There is a standing figure of General John Pershing, the commander of American forces in France in the First World War. Born in Missouri in 1860, Pershing graduated from West Point .in 1886. He fought at Wounded Knee, Cuba, and the Philippines before leading the attack on Pancho Villa in Mexico in 1916. Appointed in 1917 commander of the American forces, he was given after his victory the extra-ordinary rank of "General of the Armies," the first person so designated. The park and statue are near the site of the temporary triumphal arch erected in his honor when he led his troops in their victory parade down Pennsylvania Avenue in September 1919.

Jacqueline Kennedy saw the role of the presidency to become uniquely connected with the arts. She had lived and studied at the Sorbonne in Paris and looked naturally toward Europe for culture. One of the most memorable occasions of the entire administration was the dinner at which Pablo Casals played publicly for the first time since his vow not to do so since Franco had come to power in Spain. The dinner was described by Leonard Bernstein, one of the attendees, "To compare with an [event] with Eisenhower was like night and day...the food is marvelous, the wines are delicious...people are laughing... out loud, telling stories, telling jokes, glad to be there."

However, in her role as first lady, she would now have to focus on what was American. She sought out what was best; she helped change what Americans thought about their own culture and about themselves. She started with choosing American couture; American women all copied her. In her work on the White House, she once again set a new fashion by filling the house with American antiques.

The furnishing of the White House had been a function of small amounts of money appropriated for each incoming president. The interior decoration even of the State Rooms on the first floor would change with the changes in fashion over the years. The largest amount made available since the rebuilding of the White House after its destruction in 1814 was spent by Chester Arthur in 1882-83 under the supervision of Louis Comfort Tiffany. He particularly worked on the Red Room, the State Dining Room, and the transverse hall. The most famous of his additions was the one a visitor saw the most—the stained glass screen between the entrance hall and the transverse hall. Charles Follen McKim, in his 1902 work on the interior in concert with Edith Carew Roosevelt, removed the famous Tiffany screen and used English architectural details from the 17th and 18th century as compatible with the building's 18th century origins.

The issue of the interior furnishing of the State Rooms arose during the Coolidge administration. Starting in the 1920s, there had been increased interest in historical restoration with the installation of period rooms in places such as the American Wing of the Metropolitan Museum in New York and Colonial Williamsburg as the best-known examples. An advisory committee headed by Harriet Barnes Pratt, heir to a Standard Oil fortune, was formed to purchase furniture but received no clear sanction. They did restore the Green Room with Hepplewhite antiques. During the FDR Administration in the 1930s, the Red Room was refurnished with new wall hangings but with mainly reproduction furniture and a small budget. Illustrating the lack of concern for its historical character, after the rebuilding of the White House under President Truman, the State Rooms were re-decorated by B. Altman in New York.

In 1961, under Jacqueline Kennedy, a program of "historical restoration" began with the assistance of collectors such as Henry Francis Du Pont, the founder of Winterthur Museum in Delaware. The State Rooms began to have a museum quality to be preserved and interpreted that has continued in subsequent administrations. An "Office of the Curator of the White House" has been established in recognition of its ongoing "museum" status.

Both the Kennedys were, moreover, interested in the issue of protecting the ambience of Lafayette Park. Jacqueline Kennedy wanted to look out on a world of beauty rather than executive office buildings to be created in a bureaucratic mold. It was in the preservation of Lafayette Park that Jacqueline Kennedy receives the most recognition. In 1962, a new set of guiding principles for federal construction were issued by JFK. They included a choice of designs "that embody the finest contemporary American architectural thought" and that "the development of an official design be avoided." The latter comment reflected the almost universal commitment to neo-classical architecture exemplified in the Federal Triangle executive departmental buildings of the 1920s and 1930s under the aegis of the Commission of Fine Arts (CFA). Coincident with this new directive, prominent members in modern art and architecture were appointed to the CFA. The requirement for a new Executive Office cluster near the White House was an opportunity to house the burgeoning Executive Offices within the context of adaptive reuse while still basing itself on the 1962 directive.

John Carl Warnecke, a Bay Area architect, carried out Kennedy's 1962 directive in an innovative way that seemed to satisfy all the interested parties. In greeting him, JFK jokingly welcomed him to Washington with the statement that it might be by his work that the presidency might be most likely to be remembered. It was true that it was the architectural results of his administration that might be his lasting legacy. The row of townhouses on the west side of Lafayette Square was preserved to serve as a façade to a high redbrick building reminiscent of Colonial Williamsburg housing the Executive Offices. The compromise was consistent with Jacqueline Kennedy's preference to maintain the 19th Century character of the square.

The building used by the Court of Claims long housed in the Renwick designed former Corcoran Gallery was also to be saved (now the Renwick Gallery of the Smithsonian Institution). It was replaced by a red brick building on the east side of Lafayette Square on the site of the old Belasco Theater (Lafayette Square Opera House) that had also been the site of the William H. Seward residence during the Civil War. Other buildings to be preserved on the east side based on their historical interest were the Dolley Madison (Richard Cutts) House at the northeast corner, and adjacent to its south the Benjamin Ogle Tayloe House; both that formerly housed the Cosmos Club.

Less known to that of the role of the Kennedy's was the contribution of Stewart and Lee Udall, then secretary of the interior, to the cultural development of Washington as one of the more lasting legacies of "that one brief shining moment known as 'Camelot'." Both Udall's were descendants of Mormon pioneers. Born in 1920 the eldest of six, Stewart grew up in a small town of St John's in Arizona; Lee grew up in the larger town of Mesa. He loved poetry and music, the latter perhaps a legacy of the Mormon emphasis on music in its religious services. The somewhat obscure composer Frederick Delius was one of Udall's favorites. While on his Mormon mission in New York City, young Udall went to all the Broadway shows. After the Second World War, Stewart returned to the University of Arizona and its Law School. Lee, born in 1922 was also one of six. Her mother, a widow, raised the children on a small pension. Despite an attack of polio when in kindergarten, Lee recovered use of her legs by dint of hard work. They met at the university.

Udall was elected as a Democrat from the district that included Tucson in 1954. Stewart Udall was an obscure Arizona congressman when, in 1959, he invited the poet Robert Frost, then Poetry Consultant to the Library of Congress, to his home for dinner. The evening was a success. Frost basked in the attention; the Udall's began to fulfill their long-standing interest in the arts and literature that had been nurtured in the unlikely soil of small town Arizona. Udall thought of how Frost might add cachet to the Kennedy inauguration. After accepting the cabinet post, Udall brought the idea to JFK who then invited Frost to participate. Invitations to attend were also extended to nearly 200 other persons eminent in the arts and humanities to attend the inaugural.

Although JFK was himself bored with concerts and high culture, "Recognition of Excellence" of the arts was to be one of the themes of the Kennedy Administration. Although it had not originally intended, the Kennedy Administration thoroughly revised the federal attitude toward the arts, transforming national cultural policy from a special interest to a public concern. It was indeed to be a new Augustan age - a golden age of poetry and power that was connected with the romantic fantasy of the Arthurian legend of Camelot.

Beyond his planned recital of *The Gift Outright*, Frost was so delighted with the opportunity to participate in the Inaugural that he volunteered to compose a poem for the inauguration, an extraordinary commitment. His poem called *Dedication* spoke presciently of "the glory of a next Augustan age...a golden age of poetry and power" The story of the old man standing in the bright sun, unable to read the new poem but then reciting in his strong voice the poem he knew, set a human tone to the inauguration. It nearly upstaged the strident presidential Cold War address. In follow-up of this connection between the Kennedy Administration and the poet, Udall began, with an "Evening with Robert Frost," at a black-tie affair at the State Department as a "President's Cabinet Artists Series." Once again, Frost rose to the occasion. Over the next few years, fifteen such programs were presented that represented a wave of culture that was the new fashion. Carl Sandburg was a natural selection; Marian Anderson another and Thornton Wilder still another. The planned invitation to Pablo Casals was upstaged by his invitation to the White House itself.

Since the Second World War, repeated federal arts initiatives had failed. Cultural opponents had attacked federal arts support as a return to the "boondoggling" of the New Deal WPA. The common assumption was that the arts were "mere luxuries," even un-American. The entire Kennedy arts initiative changed the attitude of the country toward such seemingly arcane arts such as poetry and gave the country additional prestige abroad. In October 1963, before his departure for Dallas, in dedicating the Frost Library at Amherst, JFK linked art with the very creation of national values. The very individuality of the artist was essential to the strength of our civilization. Ever the Cold War Warrior, JFK vowed it was western culture that distinguished us from our adversary.

He also re-opened the long stalled drive for building a National Cultural Center near the Lincoln Memorial along the Potomac River.

There the initiative stood when his assassination interrupted any progress toward implementing these principles. Arising out of this evolution during the Kennedy years, in September 1965, LBJ signed legislation to establish the National Endowments for the Arts and the Humanities to provide federal funding for these activities.

Figure 20 - Kennedy Center for the Performing Arts

It is particularly fitting therefore for the Kennedy Center for the Performing Arts on the Potomac River was to be an appropriate memorial to John F Kennedy. Initially planned to be a National Cultural Center, it was later named after the assassinated president whose bust by Robert Berks is in the center of the Grand Foyer. The work of Edward Durrell Stone, it was a much enlarged version of his highly acclaimed American Embassy in New Delhi. Its enlargement to encompass three separate auditoriums (Concert Hall, Opera House, and Theater) overwhelms the narrow bronze exterior columns. The architect essentially maintained the character of Washington buildings as "white buildings in a park-like setting."

Furnishings and art for the Kennedy Center were gifts from the entire world in honor of its namesake. The chandeliers are Austrian; tapestries by Matisse from France; a sculpture by Barbara Hepworth from Britain; theater curtains from Japan, and a sculpture of Cervantes from Spain. Most memorable are two sculptures by Jurgen Weber from Germany placed in the Entrance Plaza. One on the west depicts *America*, particularly New York, as a canyon between skyscrapers in which there are monster cars with huge teeth for grilles, the façade of St Patrick's is wedged between glass and steel and the Statue of Liberty is engulfed in flames and smoke. Further east is another panel entitled *War or Peace*. On the left is the city smoldering surrounded by scenes of a person in an underground bunker while the city burns above. To the right is a scene of a family, nude couples kissing and Louis Armstrong playing music.

The Kennedy Center was not merely for the Washington area but was designed to have a national constituency to justify the Federal contribution. After its completion in 1972, it contained the Concert Hall for the National Symphony Orchestra; the Opera House to house the Washington National Opera as well as the Eisenhower Theater. It contains homage to President Kennedy in recognition of the increased emphasis on the arts during his administration; there are also quotations from Kennedy's speeches dealing with the significance of the arts in American life.

The Smithsonian National Air and Space Museum

Figure 21 - Smithsonian National Air and Space Museum

No less than the others, the legacy of JFK relates to the concept of what has become the favorite museum in the entire world. In 1961, in the context of the Cold War, JFK committed the United States to what no one had yet done. By the end of the decade, America would place a man on the moon. Indeed in July 1969, it would come to pass.

In the context of the Second World War, the National Air Museum was founded in 1946 in a small shed adjacent to L'Enfant Plaza and the Smithsonian Castle. Over the years, the many airplanes of that war had accumulated. Rockets and space vehicles had been created as well. The old Civil War Armory Hospital site on the Mall became the site for the present day hanger-like building that opened on the Mall in the 1970's. There are a number of spacecraft, but the history of manned flight remains an American story. There is the lone aviator of the "Spirit of St Louis"; the epitome at the very center of its entrance.

The Smithsonian Institution claims that the National Air and Space Museum (NASM), has had a long connection with itself. It claims its collection goes back to its second Secretary Spencer Baird who started its collection of Chinese kites following the 1876 Philadelphia Exhibition. Moreover, the history of aerial flight in the United States continued in the late 19th century under the aegis of the then Smithsonian Secretary Samuel Langley. The latter was a leading astronomer, the head of the Allegheny Observatory and Professor at the Western University of Pennsylvania (present-day University of Pittsburgh).

One of many over the years from the story of Icarus to Leonard da Vinci to others in Britain and France, Langley had actually in 1896 succeeded in catapulting a steam-powered pilotless "aerodrome" from a naval craft flying about a mile along the Potomac River. Then Assistant Secretary of the Navy Theodore Roosevelt encouraged Langley, and money was provided for another version of a gasoline powered model that failed on several efforts in 1903. Langley died in 1906, an object of ridicule for his expensive failure. Attempts made to rehabilitate him by the Smithsonian to the detriment of the priority of the Wright Brothers served to prevent the latter from first providing their model to the NASM.

The subsequent history of manned flight diverged far from the Smithsonian. In May 1899, the two brothers who ran a bicycle shop in Dayton Ohio had contacted the Smithsonian for copies of any information available as to human flight. Wilbur and Orville Wright were mechanically inclined, sons of a United Brethren minister. Fairly successful bicycle manufacturers, they financed their efforts on their own limited budget. Dayton was an extraordinary place; the home of the National Cash Register Company and many other such mechanical businesses. It than had the largest number of inventions per capita.

The Smithsonian made available to the Wright Brothers an English translation of a book by Louis Pierre Mouillard called *L'Empire de l'Air*. It suggested the value of studying birds in order to learn how man might fly. Orville Wright had begun to study the local birds near Dayton. In search of a place with sufficient winds to test gliders, they discovered a site on the Outer Banks of North Carolina. Their experiments with a hang glider began in testing the effects of the wind on equilibrium in October 1900. On October 19th, they each first flew several times at Kill Devil Hills near Kitty Hawk,

In a speech delivered at the Western Society of Engineers entitled "Some Aeronautical Experiments," in September 1901, Wilbur delivered the sum of his findings based on their learning of how to counter winds by warping the wings of their glider. Then with the use of a wind tunnel, the brothers demonstrated the proper wing curvatures derived from their own experimental work. On their third annual visit to Kitty Hawk, during the fall of 1902, the brothers felt that they had solved the problems of wind control. Now, only the issue of an appropriate motor remained. The propeller required still another invention since no adequate data were available for its use. With knowledge of the failure of the Langley "Grand Aerodrome," on the Potomac on December 9th, Orville was to be the first to pilot an airplane on Thursday, December 17th, 1903. The first flight lasted only 120 feet lasting 12 seconds. In a series of flights that day, the two took turns. Wilbur eventually flew as long as 852 feet for a full 59 seconds. After many more tests in a field near Dayton; back at Kitty Hawk, reporters had begun to appear to watch their flights. On October 8th, 1908, his first demonstration would take place in Le Mans France. A new age had dawned.

Although the Wright Brothers were first acclaimed in Europe as the epitome of what was so characteristically "The American," they were at first less acclaimed in the United States. It is appropriate that Neil Armstrong on his flight in July 1969 carried a bit from the original Wright Brothers' "Flyer" with him when an American then first landed on the moon.

The Civil Right Act of 1964

The 1962 mid-term election had brought a more liberal cast to the Senate. As the "in-party," the Democrats did well by losing only four seats in the House, far better than the usual in an off-year election by the governing party. The Republican counter to the young, urbane JFK was a weekly televised press conference that was lampooned as the "Ev and Charlie Show." Everett Dirksen was the Minority Leader and Charlie Halleck was the Minority Leader of the House. In this 88th Congress, there was the possibility of creating a liberal supra-partisan majority of both non-Southern Democrats and moderate and sometimes liberal Republicans. A key member of the Republican coalition was William McCullogh of Ohio

Just prior to JFK's death, the House Judiciary Committee under liberal Democrat Emmanuel Celler with the ranking Republican William McCulloch sent his Civil Rights Bill HR 3130 to the House Rules Committee. McCulloch was from a district in Ohio with few blacks. Yet he helped maintain crucial Republican support for this Civil Rights Bill and is widely credited with helping it to eventual passage without amendment. What was required was the commitment to not trade off portions as it went along but to go for cloture in breaking the likely Southern filibuster.

Yet by June 1963, it was becoming apparent to the conservative wing of the Republican presidential party that the future of the Republican Party was its principled opposition to federal intervention, albeit theoretically on non-racial grounds. Its future could be to become "The White Man's Party." Senator Barry Goldwater was the only Republican to vote against cloture on the Civil Rights Bill when it did come up under President Lyndon Johnson in the summer of 1964.

Figure 22 - William McCulloch

Born in Holmesville in western Ohio in 1901, William McCulloch trained at the College at Wooster and Ohio State College of Law. Active in Republican politics, he was minority leader of the Ohio legislature during the 1930's. A veteran of the Second World War, he was first elected to the House in 1947. In 1960, he was elected from Ohio's 4th District for his seventh term by attending his customary round of country fairs. During the previous several sessions, as the ranking Republican on the House Judiciary Committee, he led the fight in the House along with the Democratic Chair the Brooklyn Democrat Emmanuel Celler. Each year civil rights bills to amend the Civil Rights Act of 1957 had gone down in defeat in the Senate in 1958, 1959 and 1960. In that process a variety of Southern stratagems occurred to successively "trade-off" concessions to get the bills passed.

On his accession to the presidency in November 1963 after the assassination of President Kennedy, President Lyndon Johnson envisioned a set of domestic initiatives that would not only dwarf anything JFK considered but rival even that of early FDR. To LBJ, the New Deal was unfinished. He recalled how FDR had welcomed him to Washington when first elected in 1938. "He was like a daddy to me."

His vision for his own presidency was far greater, unveiled in his State of the Union Address in January 1964. It was for a "Great Society," which would provide not only an end to poverty and racial injustice but one in which there would be boundless educational opportunities for all. "His method for accomplishing this would be, as he had learned in the Senate, negotiation by give-and-take between the responsible parties. However, he could not understand securing popular assent to his policies and, ultimately national unity,

LBJ was at heart a New Deal Populist who believed that all problems could be solved by putting a floor under wages and farm prices, bringing cheap electricity to all citizens, enacting a system of universal health care, and guaranteeing an education up to graduate school. These were givens, not subject to argument; the method to accomplish this was to maintain the supra-partisan center in Congress.

The Civil Rights Bill sat at the door of the House Rules Committee at the time of the Kennedy assassination. LBJ took command quickly. The bill reached the House floor at the end of January 1964 and was passed by February 10th. Howard Smith, the conservative chair of the Rules Committee, was not able to prevent its passage. A long time partisan for women's rights, he was instrumental in the insertion of Title VII that included protection against sex discrimination with far reaching consequences for women's rights.

LBJ as president, along with Hubert Humphrey in charge of keeping the liberals in line, took personal control in the Senate. He would try to develop a supra-partisan "congressional party" by cultivating the Republican Everett Dirksen to bypass the southern Democrats and break up the conservative coalition. Senator Russell of Georgia was the leader of the filibuster of the Southern Democrats along with the Republican Texan Senator John Tower. After 57 working days, the cloture vote was taken with 67 votes to end debate.

It was unclear as to the ability as well as the commitment of the Republican leader to the civil rights vote. Most of the mid-west Republicans in his group had few black constituents. Unlike previous times, the commitment made to McCulloch in the House did not permit trading away provisions in return for passage. However, with the aid of 27 Republicans, cloture to limit debate was passed by the two-thirds vote necessary. Dirksen was enabled to make face-saving cosmetic changes while being heaped with praise for his statesmanlike actions. Its passage had taken a year since it had first been introduced by JFK. LBJ signed the bill on July 2nd, 1964 in the East Room of the White House prior to adjournment for the nominating conventions.

The Civil Rights Act of 1964 replicated in its Title I unequal application of obstacles to voting; Title II discrimination in access to hotels etc; Title III discrimination by government; Title IV accords access to help by the U.S. Attorney General to litigation and in Title V amplification of the powers of the U.S. Civil Rights Commission. Title VII has had particular implication by assuring equality based on gender. Among those surrounding LBJ at its signing was Martin Luther King, Whitney Young of the Urban League. George Meany of the AF of L-CIO, William Halleck, Emmanuel Celler and William McCulloch of Ohio.

LBJ hoped to dispose of the unfinished Kennedy agenda that was pending in Congress prior to the start of the 1964 election. The Civil Rights Bill passed in July 1964 could be seen as unfinished business left over from the Kennedy Administration; the Economic Opportunity Bill passed in August could be seen as new business. The issue of poverty had begun to come to Kennedy's attention during his 1960 presidential campaign in Appalachia and was discussed as benefiting whites even more than blacks. But JFK had not yet acted; President Johnson did so. Unlike other initiatives in health and education that had been discussed in Congress for many years and had already well-established coalitions, the War on Poverty arose as an Executive initiative. Moreover, it was Johnson's first new personal initiative. He used it as an example of his true colors as a New Dealer and to disprove any intimation that he was more conservative than his predecessor. It was also seen, in the spirit of the Peace Corps, to arouse the idealism of the youth of the country.

Figure 23 - Everett Dirksen

Born into a Republican German immigrant family, Everett Dirksen's middle name was McKinley. He went to University of Minnesota before leaving to join the army in the First World War. Active in the American Legion, he was also involved in the local dramatic society. A highly conservative congressman from the area near Peoria Illinois from 1933 onward, he became Senator in 1950 and minority leader in 1959. Throughout his career in Congress, his role was to be in opposition. He also came from the district once represented by Abraham Lincoln and was a warm friend of Lyndon Johnson with whom he had worked closely when the latter was majority leader with a Republican president.

As a southerner, LBJ hoped that his fellow southerners would understand and support his diversion from a more purely racial to an economic view of solving the problems of the racial divide. Since LBJ was acting almost entirely on presidential initiative; his ultimate failure illustrates the limits of such initiatives. LBJ's 1964 Economic Opportunity Act concentrated on dealing with the culture of poverty; on job creation, not welfare checks. It created the Job Corps that provided training for unemployed teenagers,(analogous to LBJ's own experience in Texas with FDR's National Youth Administration

(NYA); and VISTA (Volunteers in Service to America), the inner-city equivalent of the Peace Corps. Legal Services for the Poor was new. Another more innovative aspect added later was Head Start, a pre-school program for the disadvantaged. The last has been longest lasting.

LBJ shrewdly chose Sargent Shriver, the founder of the Peace Corps and a Kennedy brother-in-law, to run the Office of Economic Opportunity (OEO). Shriver had the distinction of being a Kennedy family member but not being Bobby Kennedy; he would indicate a Kennedy connection but permit the Johnson imprint on the new agency. Moreover, OEO would transmit its funds through local "Community Action Programs" (CAPS). This aspect incorporated a significantly new idea that had arisen during the Kennedy Administration in the Department of Justice. Its beginning was the focus on community rather than individual origins of poverty and the importance of a "bottoms-up" approach to its solution. Michael Harrington's 1962 book *The Other America* emphasized both the extent and persistence of what could be termed a *culture* of poverty.

A comprehensive community approach to its mitigation also arose from ongoing thinking within Robert Kennedy's (and Eunice Kennedy Shriver's) interest in juvenile delinquency and community gangs. The Community Action concept resonated with LBJ but its acceptance was delayed based on its origins in Robert Kennedy's Justice Department. However, LBJ did not want to be accused of betraying the Kennedy legacy so soon.

The Election of 1964

Reaching for a theme that would encompass his vision at University of Michigan in May 1964. "We now have the opportunity to move not only toward a rich society and a powerful society, but toward a Great Society." The choice of site was conditioned by its use by JFK to launch his "Peace Corps" concept during the 1960 election campaign. The theme would resonate not only with that of American history in its quest for "the pursuit of happiness," but with the energy and activism of the times; to do something not just more but somehow greater by it being different and better. Based on the sense of abundance, the goal was to give people a greater opportunity to participate in that abundance.

The more moderate "establishment" wing of the Republican Party, to its surprise, failed to control the Republican national convention. Their candidate Nelson Rockefeller was not chosen. Although patently unpopular in the country as a whole, Barry Goldwater was the candidate of the more extremist right wing of the party. The election was won on many fronts; not the least of which was the famous spot ad showing the little girl counting off the petals of the flower ending in a boom. Television spot ads, particularly negative ones, became an ever-present fixture of all subsequent political campaigns.

While going down to defeat in the general election, the seeds were planted for the Republican resurgence. Its new base was to be strident anti-Communism, the White Man's party in the North as well as the South, conservative social values of the second generation ethnics and, not incidentally, unfettered laissez-faire economics.

The landslide election of LBJ over Barry Goldwater also led to an enlargement of the Democratic control of Congress. In the fabled 89th Congress, the Democrats held 295 seats in the House and 68 in the Senate. A supra-partisan centrist coalition was thus possible. John McCormack remained Speaker, Carl Albert was majority leader and Hale Boggs was majority whip. Gerald Ford from Michigan became minority leader replacing the more irascible Charlie Halleck. Nevertheless, several Republicans were elected from the former Confederacy for the first time since Reconstruction, a harbinger of the future.

LBJ recalled the short window of opportunity available to FDR after his own landslide of 1936. The president wasted no time in the winter of 1965. Right after Bloody Sunday on the Selma Alabama Bridge in March 1965, LBJ reached his pinnacle of power but also of righteousness when he called on all Americans, both north and south, to overcome the legacy of bigotry and injustice as it affected the basic right to vote. At the end of his peroration, he electrified the Congress and the country when he added the code words of the anthem of the civil rights movement "and we… shall… overcome."

The Civil Rights Act of 1964 dealt with public accommodation and fair employment practices but not the fundamental issue of voter registration. The conditions were opportune. There was a large Democratic majority due to the election of 1964; the press on the streets of Selma was there and the Republicans under Dirksen were still supportive. The Voting Rights Bill of 1965 suspended literacy tests and other obstacles. LBJ saw himself after the election of 1964 as the heir of an "Era of Good Feeling," comparable to that of James Monroe. LBJ regarded his vast majority against Goldwater as a permanent base of support. Partisan, ideological and factional disputes would give way to serene consensus presided over by LBJ. His magic that had worked while he was master of the Senate seemed to work now that he was president. He was on the phone constantly, cajoling, persuading, seducing, coercing.

Moreover, it was a time when the civil rights movement was energizing the breakup of the past hundred years of segregation that had seemed inviolate. LBJ's speech, introducing his Voting Rights bill in March 1965 reached his greatest heights of eloquence in its acknowledgement of the theme of that movement. Writing what would be LBJ's greatest speech, Richard Goodwin reflected in viewing the recent scenes of brutality at Selma his own childhood experience as a Jew of "the fear of my youth…at the approach of muscular men whose faces were contorted by hate."

The Senate Judiciary Committee was chaired by the segregationist Alabama Senator Eastland, but was operating under a two-week rule. After the usual filibuster, cloture could take place. After being blocked by Howard Smith, the Bill was also dislodged from the House Rules Committee by the threat by Emanuel Celler, chair of the Judiciary Committee, to invoke the 21-day rule limiting delay by that body. The Voting Rights Act was signed into law in August 1965. The Act contained the provision for the insertion of federal registrars in districts that were particularly problematic. Black voter registration rose significantly in the South, blacks were elected as Democrats to the House from selected districts but statewide and presidential elections went to the majority whites who voted Republican.

This far-reaching Act was part of the crest of the Hundred Days of the 89th Congress that also included the passage of Medicare, Medicaid, and the formation of the Department of Housing and Urban Development (HUD).

The June 1965 Howard University commencement address went even further. LBJ introduced the concept of *affirmative action* to make up for the years of being hobbled by racial prejudice. Beyond desegregation, the movement was for integration of black Americans into the mainstream of life. The program for the implementation of this Second Reconstruction had been laid out. But so had the "white backlash" in the north represented by the candidacy of George Wallace.

There were still other possibilities in the heady first half of 1965. The great accomplishment of the expansion of the principle of Social Security to health care had lain unfulfilled; the idea had been nurtured by men such as Wilbur Cohen since the passage of the original Social Security Act in 1935.

Cohen worked at a technical level for the Committee of Economic Security (CES) under his old professor from Madison. Over the years of the New Deal and its successors, he was involved at various levels in the development of the basic legislation; aided in its passage in Congress in 1935. He aided in its implementation as the protégé of Arthur Altmeyer, the head of the Social Security program; and the piece meal expansion of Social Security in terms of scope and categories of workers covered. Cohen continued to be central to those thinking during the Eisenhower years as a member of the faculty at the University of Michigan School of Social Work. He returned to Washington in 1960 as a high official of JFK's Department of HEW.

Passage of a health insurance as an addition to Social Security had become possible. Wilbur Mills was central to the latter. Cohen, always friendly with Mills, served as his technical adviser in preparing the bill that was passed in July 1965. Cohen considered Medicare the legislative achievement of his life. Now, Undersecretary of HEW, he was responsible for its relatively smooth implementation, ensuring the desegregation of health facilities in the South as a byproduct. He finally became Secretary of HEW in 1968 in the waning days of the LBJ Administration.

Figure 24 - Wilbur Cohen

Wilbur Cohen was born in 1913 of scholarly East European immigrants in Milwaukee. As a child of the Great Jewish Migration, he departed from his origins during his personal life but not during his career. The Depression and the need for the alleviation of economic insecurity formed his world view. He was part of the rise to the professional class and positions of influence during the New Deal of the sons of the Jewish migration. Trained in labor economics at the University of Wisconsin, he joined the large number of Progressives in the burgeoning New Deal agencies in Washington.

The passage of Medicare in the Senate was aided by Russell Long on the Senate Finance Committee. Long, of the Huey Long dynasty of Louisiana, was able to bypass the adamant opposition of Virginia's Democratic Senator Byrd on the Finance Committee. The latter, the stalwart since the 1930s of the conservative coalition, was always opposed to government expenditures. In the House, Wilbur Mills, chair of the Ways and Means Committee, surprisingly created the broad "three-layer" bill that seemed to meet all the various proposals afoot from the Republicans, the "American Medical Association" (AMA) as well as the Administration. The Bill included the hospital benefit of Part A paid through Social Security taxes, the medical benefit of Part B paid for by its recipients as well as general tax revenues and the low-income Part C of Medicaid.

Passed by July 1965, the Act was signed by LBJ in the Truman Library in the presence of the earlier president. That gesture was in recognition of President Truman's earlier unsuccessful proposal for health care under Social Security and the even earlier 1935 proposal by Senator Wagner when Social Security was first enacted. The idea of National Health Insurance was acceptable if limited to the elderly.

Aid to education had not yet been accomplished until LBJ's Great Society and the election of 1964. The latter was beset by Southern concerns about desegregation with federal intrusion into education, heretofore under local control. There was also opposition from Catholics intent on receiving support for their schools, a delicate problem for the Catholic President JFK. With the succession of LBJ and the window of opportunity offered by the election of 1964, the passage of the education bills was accomplished.

The formation of what finally became the Department of Housing and Urban Development (HUD) had been first proposed by JFK in the spring of 1961. It was billed in moderate non-racial bureaucratic terms as a mere reorganization. Controversy arose based on the widespread premise that Robert Weaver would be designated the first secretary. Head of the Housing and Housing Finance Agency (HHFA), he would be an appropriate appointee if he were not an African-American. Once his likely selection was publicly stated in October 1961, Southern opposition became entrenched on the Housing Committees of both branches of Congress. The Bill was defeated in February 1962.

Figure 25 - Robert C Weaver

Robert C Weaver's entire career was closely associated with the issue of housing. Born in 1907, he was a product of the Washington middle-class black community. His great-grandfather, having purchased his own freedom in 1842, his maternal grandfather was the first black to graduate from Harvard University in dentistry. Weaver was educated at Dunbar High School, the top public high school in the Washington, DC segregated system before going to Harvard himself. Weaver eventually received his doctorate there in economics in 1933.

Unlike the past group of token jobs that were reserved for blacks primarily as political patronage, positions were created in the New Deal to affect policy. Brought in as the black assistant to the white "Special Advisor on Negro Affairs" at the Department of the Interior, Weaver was soon promoted in 1934 to full position as the Advisor on Negro Affairs to Harold Ickes. He was also a leading member of the unofficial "Black Cabinet," to be called upon to deal with racial issues. Weaver chose the housing program of the Public Works Administration (PWA) under Ickes as his specialty.

The first intrusion of federal funds into this area, it provided him an opportunity to introduce non-discrimination employment clauses based on "quotas," a new idea at the time. Segregation in the assignment of public housing units was unquestioned. In providing much needed housing for blacks, racial segregation was entrenched even where it had not previously existed. With the formation in 1937 of the "United States Housing Authority" (USHA), Weaver moved to the new agency in a job similar to the one he had at Interior but now clearly primarily focused on housing issues.

In 1960, JFK offered him the opportunity to run the "Housing and Home Financing Agency" (HHFA). He was the highest ranking African-American in the federal government. At the tail end of his great summer of achievement in 1965, LBJ reinstated the plan to establish a Department of Housing and Urban Affairs with Weaver as its first secretary. The original title of "Department of the Cities" was considered too radical. In light of the disturbances of the summer of 1965 in places like Watts just after the passage of the Voting Rights Act, LBJ envisaged that the new department would go beyond the coordinating bureaucratic role as outlined by JFK. More than slum clearance and public housing, the goal was to improve the health of cities, their social fabric. Related to racial unrest, the appointment of the first African-American to a cabinet post was part of the symbolic message that LBJ sought.

The sound of broken glass and of laughter as clothes and television sets were being hauled out of stores from Lenox Avenue in Harlem reverberated on televisions in the homes of Americans everywhere occurred in the first of the 1964 summer riots. The response for many was the "white backlash." But for many summers to come, Harlem was set an example, the very month the Civil Rights Act was signed, in the summer and the subsequent summers to come.

Still another riot took place as the very campaign of 1964 was taking place at the verdant campus of the University of California at Berkeley. The explosion was taking place because of the campaign itself. Under prodding by Senator William Knowland, publisher of the nearby *Oakland Tribune*, all political campaigning was forbidden on campus. A "united front" took place of all the political groups on campus that ignited into the "Free Speech Movement" that ended in the firing of the school chancellor in vindication of the students. Their leader had been moved by his earlier experience in the civil rights movement. These young were the cutting edge of the Baby Boom generation born to post-war America. Opposition to Viet Nam was not yet in their slogans; that was to come.

The United States was going through one of the hinges in its history. Confidence in the underpinnings of a government that had accepted the segregation of American life imposed by the fire hoses of Birmingham were exposed for their rottenness. In the same month of May 1963 as that of Birmingham, Americans also watched on their televisions They had wanted to believe that the country that had worked to free people from evils such as Nazism was working to help free people become free from a colonial regime in Viet Nam exposed by the self-immolation of Buddhist monks. They could not believe that America was supporting an unpopular regime in South Viet Nam. A regime that was so unpopular with its Buddhist monks who were prepared to burn themselves in opposition to it.

Driven by his grandiloquence, LBJ envisioned the need to proceed with his domestic program despite the increased commitment to the Viet Nam War starting up significantly in 1965. Rather than call up the reserves and the National Guard, LBJ elected to continue the draft to fill out the expanded needs of the military build-up in Viet Nam. This was not, after all, a major war on the home front. It was also LBJ's hope that the war would soon be over. Not even 1% of the over 500,000 men in Viet Nam by the end of his presidency were reserves and National Guard. Businessmen still run their businesses, and college kids still go to college. The worst of the war was being beamed into middle class living rooms; the blood and gore and the atrocities. It tore the country from the heart of the military and tore the military from the heart of the country.

Bound by his $100 billion self-imposed budget, LBJ vowed to not ask for a tax increase to help pay for the growing war. He could not get the guns to win victory nor the budget for the butter to gain the victory in the Great Society program he really needed. The latter was his primary goal. The legislative agenda for the second year of the Great Society for which Joseph Califano was responsible would deal with the problems of the urban ghettoes that had recently exploded.

Figure 26 - Joseph A. Califano, Jr.

Joseph A. Califano, Jr was an only child in 1931 to a Catholic family in Brooklyn. His Irish mother was thought to be marrying beneath herself by her far more Americanized and genteel family. His father was an extremely faithful long time clerical employee of IBM, his mother a teacher in the public schools. Young Califano grew up in Catholic schools taught by strict nuns immersed in a family life imbued with ritualistic religious observance. He lived in Crown Heights but saw himself defined by living in St Gregory's parish, more genteel than neighboring St Theresa's parish.

The 89th Congress elected in the 1964 landslide continued to be responsive.

The "Model Cities" initiative was designed to make urban renewal less that of black removal, more sensitive to the needs of those affected. However, its passage was caught up in the controversy of the Community Action provisions of the Economic Opportunity Act. Somewhat less controversial than the latter, the Model Cities program was also more circumspect in intruding onto the turf of the local politicians. Still, its "open housing" integrated housing provisions were a sticking point.

His mother worked hard to erase any vestiges of a Brooklyn accent; his father enforced a correct dress code. He went to the prestigious Brooklyn Prep in preparation for the Jesuit College of the Holy Cross in Worcester Massachusetts. He maintained his Catholicism while adding to it his entry into the more sophisticated secular world of the Harvard Law School. He proved himself by qualifying in his second year for the *Harvard Law Review*. After service in the Navy, with his contacts from Harvard, he too entered the golden door leading to an old-line Wall Street law firm.

Caught up in the 1960 Kennedy campaign, Califano left Wall Street to become one of the "whiz kids" at the Pentagon under Robert McNamara as the first generation of Italian Catholic ethnics. He entered the direct orbit of LBJ in July 1965 to replace Bill Moyers, now about to become press secretary. Califano was the person responsible for coordinating the multiple aspects of the LBJ domestic agenda. Despite the impact of Viet Nam, he persisted. Coming from his own background imbued with the Jesuit teaching of anti-materialism, he appreciated the moral basis of the Johnson agenda and worked for its acceptance in Congress. He saw himself, in fact, doing the Lord's Work consistent with the 1961 encyclical of Pope John XXIII.

The "Glorious 89th Congress" came to its end. LBJ had also created the "National Endowment for the Arts" (NEA) and "National Endowment for the Humanities" (NEH) as well as funding the Kennedy Center for the Performing Arts. Before the end of his term, LBJ had also begun National Public Radio (NPR). LBJ permitted himself to compare the results of his Great Society to that of the New Deal, and to compare himself to his original hero FDR. LBJ had indeed stressed the alleviation of human suffering but had embraced a far more sweeping agenda and had encouraged grass roots participation and the entry of blacks into partnership in the ruling councils of the Democratic Party, very different from that of FDR's New Deal.

The Election of 1966

The Viet Nam War had heated up. Right after his entry to office, LBJ had warned his advisors that "he was not going to be the president who saw southeast Asia go the way that China went." He was acutely aware that the story of "losing China" had destroyed the ability of President Truman to pursue his "Fair Deal." LBJ did not want the loss of Southeast Asia to be the undoing of his own "Great Society." Carrying out his overall plan required him not to lose in Viet Nam. The first step was the "Rolling Thunder" bombing campaign to bomb Hanoi; next to introduce ground troops; then more of the latter so that by the end of 1965 there were nearly 400,000 U.S. troops in Viet Nam. Still colored by Wilsonian sentiments, LBJ gave a speech in the spring of 1965 about building a Mekong Delta TVA-type program to solve the problems of South Viet Nam.

Following the landslide presidential election of FDR in 1936, so again there was a recrudescence of the seemingly dormant Republican Party in the mid-term election of 1966. The Republicans regained forty-six seats in the 90th Congress that they had lost in 1964. The conservative coalition was once again in control of the House; the 21-day rule was repealed that had enabled liberal legislation to reach the floor from the obstructionist House Rules Committee. Moreover, there were Republican gains in both the House and Senate from the formerly solidly Democratic South. Spiro Agnew was elected Republican governor of Democratic state of Maryland, albeit on a less racist ticket than his Democratic opponent.

After 1966, there were but 156 Northern Democrats; there were under Mansfield a less than lukewarm support for the war in Viet Nam in the Senate. Although far more blacks were able to vote and were able to elect local officials such as sheriffs, the fruits of the Voting Rights Act of 1965 were translated into a larger number of Southern whites voting Republican. The Republican Southern strategy as the "White Man's party" had begun to pay off.

In February 1966, after the fruitless Christmas bombing pause, LBJ agreed to push the troop commitment to over 400,000 leading to endless protests. In May 1966 nearly one-third of voters were opposed to keeping our troops in Viet Nam. This is to be contrasted with the near unanimous support after Pearl Harbor and even in Korea despite dissatisfaction with that war. Finally, the "success" of the Viet Nam Tet Offensive in February 1967 seemed to confirm the loss of will. Victory was an acceptable response; so was withdrawal. What was not acceptable, as it turned out to be, was a bloody stalemate.

Inflation started in light of LBJ's predilection for both "guns and butter" as the war in Viet Nam continued to heat up. Nevertheless, even real GNP increased over and above inflation each year during the 1960's. The business cycle had seemingly been abolished. The jobs were becoming more frequently white collar; they required more verbal skills and more education. There were also the continued riots in the urban ghettos of Cleveland, Chicago and New York City and the unrest on the campuses such as Berkeley. The New Left questioned the very premises of LBJ's vision. Their criticism extended beyond his Viet Nam policy to the very idea of larger centralized government. LBJ, concerned about being attacked by the right wing extremists for being "soft on communism," was also liable to criticism for abandoning the Catholics of South Viet Nam. He failed to understand how the thousands on the streets of Washington represented the extension to the wider population of the stirrings on the left. The Great Society could not fulfill its promises and seemingly, no new initiatives were possible.

It appeared particularly unlikely that any housing anti-discrimination bill would pass in light of the continued political unrest in the North. Thanks to intense lobbying by Clarence Mitchell of the NAACP and the support of several dedicated senators, cloture was finally achieved, now despite the efforts of Senator Dirksen. In the House, efforts by the real estate industry were thwarted by the acceptance of the Senate bill. The much weakened Civil Rights Bill of 1968 ended discrimination in housing in the overwhelming majority of units for sale or rental. Immediately after the assassination of Martin Luther King, crowning the Civil Rights Acts of 1964, 1965, President Lyndon Johnson had helped with the Civil Rights Act of 1968 to bring about this -his second effort at Reconstruction.

What had been lost was not only the war in Viet Nam and the loss of opportunity to truly "make America a great multi-racial society," What was being lost was the faith that even "the best and the brightest" that had taken power in 1960 had fallen short. The remainder of the century would be spent in dealing with their degree of both success and failure.

The Legacy in Washington DC of President Lyndon Johnson

In 1932, a poll asked 50 leading architects to rate buildings "whose architectural design was felt to be most satisfactory." Those selected in Washington included the Lincoln Memorial, the Scottish Rite Temple on 16th Street, the Folger Shakespeare Library on Capitol Hill and the Freer Gallery of Art on the National Mall. Unlike New York and other cities where the buildings selected were almost entirely buildings modern in style, those selected within Washington were all variants of the Classical revival style. They were an indication of the degree to which a commitment to Classicism permeated the city. As late as the 1940's, the influence of the McMillan Commission and the CFA helped to maintain its conservative architectural character in the West Gallery of the National Gallery of Art (1941) and the Jefferson Memorial (1943). During the 1930s and 1940s, Classicism persisted in Federal Buildings, maintaining classical building composition and massive but devoid of ornamentation, known as "Stripped Classicism" or "Depression Moderne" used for many of the New Deal buildings

The National Museum of American History (initially called the Museum of History and Technology) was designed by the successor to the firm of McKim, Mead and White in the 1950s. It was the first of the new Post-Second World War Smithsonian Museums on the National Mall between 12th and 14th Streets. The building was conceived as a modernized version of the temple format of the Lincoln Memorial. Regularly spaced slabs of concrete replicate the more traditional columns. The collection in this museum replicates the eclectic character of the earliest National Museum in the Patent Office in its range from the ruby red shoes worn by Judy Garland in the *Wizard of Oz* to the Woolworth lunch counter in Greensboro North Carolina where the first sit-in took place in 1960.

The political climate toward modernism in this post-Second World War era remained hostile. The chairman of the House Committee on Public Buildings considered the "-isms" (surrealism, Dadaism, cubism) of modern art as foreign imports that represented depravity and destruction. The continuing battle to place modern, more abstract, art within the monumental core was seen as a battle between conservative and more experimental even iconoclastic political philosophies as well as lifestyles. An abstract sculpture called *Infinity* was placed in 1967 in front of the building of the Museum of American History, the first abstract sculpture commissioned by the Federal Government in Washington. A Calder stabile called *Gwenfritz* in honor of its donor Gwendolyn Cafritz was placed near the west front of that same building. The Sculpture Gardens attached to the Hirschhorn and the Sculpture Garden of the National Gallery of Art (the latter also donated by the Cafritz Foundation) now display a range of modern art.

There had long been an interest in contemporary art being displayed on the Mall. A design by Eliel and Eero Saarinen (father and son) in 1939 for an American art museum with its asymmetrical design, long ribbon windows and the flat roof characteristic of the "International Style" had never been built. It deviated from the accepted standard for governmental architecture of that time. There was particular opposition from the Commission of Fine Arts (CFA). By the 1960s, there was no longer the original commitment to the neo-classical Beaux Arts tradition established by the McMillan Commission and carried out by the CFA. In the post-war era, this pre-war design for an American art museum on the Mall was reconsidered and indeed approved by a far different CFA but not built.

The elder Saarinen was a Finnish architect noted for his work in the United States starting in the 1920s at the Cranbrook School of Art in Bloomfield Michigan. The son Eero went on in the post-Second World War era to build the Gateway Arch in St Louis as well as the Dulles International Airport in Northern Virginia.

The completion of the ensemble of museums along the National Mall now diverged from roots in classical Europe. Instead of making the federal city worthy of the nation, the commitment was now to be worthy of the world. A site on the south side of the Mall was made open by the destruction of the redbrick Army Medical Museum designed by Adolph Cluss. Gordon Bunshaft was one of the leading architects of the time, partner in the firm of Skidmore, Owings, and Merrill, and a member of the CFA. He had already been selected by President Lyndon Johnson to design the Johnson Library at the University of Texas. The Hirschhorn's circular concrete design helped break up the line of the adjacent rectangular Air and Space Museum to its east. Like a piece of modern sculpture, the Hirschhorn Museum at 8th Street and Independence Avenue is aggressively modern in its appearance. It reflects the avant-garde art it houses but contrasts with the restrained Italian Renaissance character of the Freer Gallery of Art on the other side of the Smithsonian Castle. It is also in rebuttal to the principles behind the monumental neo-classical National Gallery of Art opposite on the Mall.

Figure 27 – Hirschhorn Museum

The Hirschhorn contains the large art collection of Joseph Hirschhorn donated in 1966. A Jewish immigrant from Latvia, he was one of 12 children who came to New York in 1905. Desperately poor, the widowed mother worked in a sweatshop in the garment industry. Short and ambitious, young Hirschhorn did well as a broker on Wall Street, In the 1930s; he parlayed his winnings into uranium mines in Canada. Interested in art since boyhood, he collected contemporary art in large quantities. He would buy up whole studios of work from artists he liked. He acquired art to suit his personal taste in contrast to the more traditional art that the Federal Government tended to support and collect. Courted by President Lyndon Johnson and Dillon Ripley, Secretary of the of the Smithsonian, to make Washington a cultural center equal to other capitals in an area of "art of our time" in which it was then lacking. It was to be Smithsonian's Museum of Modern and Contemporary Art. The collection was given to the country and the eponymous museum completed in 1974.

Figure 28 - East Gallery of the National Gallery of Art

Even more exemplary has been the work of I.M. Pei in his East Gallery of the National Gallery of Art. So different from the original Beaux-Arts West Gallery of the National Gallery of Art, the triangular East Gallery, completed in 1978, is in the spirit of the aborted pre-Second World War Saarinen design and a reflection of the opportunities now offered for modernism in Washington. Its design is derived from its triangular plot of land but also in the modern idiom to provide space appropriate for contemporary art. The museum portion is composed of two isosceles triangles coming to a focus in the center of the skylight, echoing the central dome of the original West Building. Its responsiveness to classicism lies in its abstract use of geometric figures. Made from the same quarry of Tennessee marble used earlier, it does not face the Mall but is directed toward its elder brother.

Despite the difference in idiom, the elegance and detail of the architecture shares that of the original as a sacred enclave dedicated to the creative achievement of individuals. The very large and well-lit interior atrium contains the huge Calder mobile; people move along stairways, escalators, and bridges. The East Gallery was designed to permit the display of the large pieces characteristic of post-war art, mainly the American abstract expressionist and subsequent schools, no longer interdicted by the original ban on living artists of the National Gallery of Art. Many are part of the collection of Robert and Jane Meyerhoff including works by Jasper John and Robert Rauschenberg among many others. Meyerhoff is a major real estate investor from Baltimore. His donation to the National Gallery of Art rather than the art museum in his own city illustrates the attraction Washington now had. This contrasts with the 19th century experience when philanthropists would endow universities elsewhere.

I.M. Pei, born in China, trained at MIT and Harvard under Walter Gropius, of Bauhaus fame. He built many buildings throughout the world in the style of Mies van der Rohe, another of the Bauhaus pioneers. His most famous building is the pyramidal entrance to the Louvre. It is said that French President Francois Mitterrand hired Pei for the Grand Louvre based on his sensitive design for the East Gallery of the National Gallery of Art.

The Viet Nam Veterans Memorial

Overshadowing even the great accomplishments of the domestic program initiated by Lyndon Johnson was the divisive and unsuccessful war that prevented the possible fulfillment of his vision for a "Great Society." The design of the Viet Nam Veterans Memorial by Maya Lin in 1982 most clearly reflected the ambiguity of the post-war world of American hegemony for it listed the names of persons rather than the names of battles. The war had lasted twenty years, starting in 1955, and had taken over 58,000 American troops.

Selected from over 1400 entries in the largest architectural competition in history, the "Wall" was funerary rather than triumphant or heroic. The American defense of South Viet Nam against a guerilla insurgency from its Communist North failed. It was the first war that the United States lost. Moreover, there had been disunion over its morality and its value. Veterans returning from what was a very difficult war was fought against guerrillas were not welcomed home. Military service was for some a mark of shame rather than the glory that had met the veterans of the Second World War.

Figure 29 - Viet Nam Veterans Memorial

A group of Viet Nam veterans led by Jan Scruggs, a former enlisted man, created the Viet Nam Veterans Memorial on the Mall to redress these issues, to encourage national healing and reconciliation. Scruggs determined that all names be there and nothing distinguishes the rank of the dead. Controversy over its design and placement of the Memorial reflected the controversy over the war itself. One learns nothing about the war's cause or purpose because the cause and purpose were unclear. On entering the valley of the dead that the Viet Nam Memorial Wall represents, the inscription is "1959 in honor of the men and women of the Armed Forces of the United States who served in the Viet Nam War. The names of those who gave their lives and those who remain missing are inscribed in the order they were taken from us."

The names and dates are inscribed on polished black granite that further contributes to the power of reflection that it creates. It ends with "Our nation honors the courage, service, and devotion to duty and country of its Viet Nam veterans..." The sentiment behind it is neither patriotic nor unpatriotic but an honoring of the boundary between the living and the dead that invites contemplation and participation from the visitor.

Tom Carhart, originally a member of the Viet Nam Memorial Commission, broke with colleagues over the choice of Lin's design, calling it a "deep gash of shame." He and others demanded something more that indicated patriotism and reverence for the country. He led a group that that commissioned Frederick Hart's *"Three Infantrymen"* just to the right of a high flagpole with the American flag placed at a slight distance from the Wall. One of the Infantrymen is portrayed as White, another African American and the third Hispanic to represent the racial diversity of the military that had occurred since the integration of the services by President Truman. In addition, in 1994, the "Viet Nam Women's Memorial" by Glenna Goodacre was added to honor the 8000 nurses who served in Viet Nam. It shows three nurses with one holding a soldier receiving help like the Madonna in the tradition of the *Pieta*. It is suggested that this amalgam of images has served to bring about the reconciliation that the Memorial sought to achieve by incorporating the commemorative wishes of several different segments of those interested.

The Great Society Subway

The story of the Washington Metro system is a story of a commuter system for travelers in and out of a central city in the mid-20th century. However, it is a story with larger implications. Other cities such as Atlanta and San Francisco also designed systems at the same time. Moreover, this city was Washington, DC. It was the national capital of a great country at a time of its greatest prosperity. For a short time, it was the time of "The Great Society." with "enough will, any goal was within reach."

Unlike other transit systems where engineering was primary and architecture clearly secondary, both were involved from the start. Moreover, the Committee of Fine Arts and its chairman Gordon Bunshaft, insisted on consistency throughout in accordance with the monumentality of the national capital. All underground stations share the barrel vaults made of coffered concrete arches and mezzanines appear to be floating structures. The earlier above ground stations follow a similar gull-wing canopy design. Its aesthetics help maintain the quality of the design.

Figure 30 - Metro Center

Acclaimed as one of the greatest public-works projects in history, it was also a sign of the diversion of resources away from the private automobile. American cities in the 20th century had grown up in the era of the automobile. The very epitome of American culture, the interstate highway had been single minded in the 1950's. The City of Tomorrow that had so excited the viewers at the New York World's Fair in 1939-1940 had come to fruition. Post the Second World War, suburbanization had indeed come about. Broad limited access highways had indeed occurred, aided by General Motors, its sponsor at the World Fair.

The city of Washington was unique. It was not a city subject only to commercial considerations. It was a national shrine that could not as easily be destroyed if its surface had become choked by the predominance of vehicular traffic. The Metro was in general largely underground within the District of Columbia and Arlington County. The city and its regions continue to grow outward and "edge cities" continue to form to be encompassed by its extension in the next generation. The Metro system did not arise *de novo*. It followed the established lines of a central city surrounded by suburbs that could be tapped by a "spike and hub" design. It followed the already established pattern of the surface transit lines created over the hundred years of the 19th century when Washington first became a city during the Civil War.

CHAPTER 5
THE YEARS OF RICHARD NIXON AND HIS SUCCESSION 1968-1976

Introduction

The riots finally came to Washington itself in the spring of the Easter assassination of Martin Luther King in 1968. As the riots had occurred throughout the country's cities, the Kerner Commission had been appointed in 1967 by LBJ after the riot in Detroit. It called for more massive federal programs to help blacks. Most voters failed to agree. MLK despaired of blacks being able to compete in a free-market economy and was flirting with socialism before his death with his "Poor People's Campaign." Far more intractable would be any fundamental redistribution in American society.

Most American voters had moved away from the politics of redistribution. The issues of the civil rights marches were cultural; it was an entry into capitalism, not its demise. While Southerners moved to the Republican Party, blacks and many other whites remained Democrats. The Viet Nam war would split the young, subject to the draft. In every outword manner, the young bearded ones were expressing in their drug-filled, sexually explicit way their disrespect and contempt for the norms of previously acceptable norms of society.

The march on the Pentagon in the fall of 1969 chronicled by Norman Mailer was not the first, nor the last or the most violent. However, it was the largest in its participation. Families came together to march; it was a march that transcended boundaries. Even the cold war warrior Paul Nitze's three children participated. LBJ complained in the midst of a diplomatic reception of the smell of tear gas filtering into the White House. There was the smell of marijuana and the different character of the break-up of the young, those going to college and those not. The break-up of the young that was evident at Ohio's Kent State.

Richard Nixon from the start of his career was one of the first politicians to recognize the significance of Asia in the Cold War. His entire career rose on the "loss of China" and the weakness of the Democrats in that effort. He could not break free from the orthodoxies of Cold War doctrine regarding the monolithic nature of world communism and the military nature of containment in the third world. Having consistently advocated a military approach to containment, he found himself presiding over American disengagement from Viet Nam in the 1970s. His slow retreat from military disengagement was one of his serious errors. Nixon's Viet Nam War was a necessary price he continued to find necessary to incur to shore up American power in the face of the "domino theory." His attempt to use Moscow and Peking to accomplish this effort failed. His detente strategy did not actually provide the groundwork for the destruction of the Soviet Union that President Reagan accomplished in the next set of efforts in the late 1980's and 1990's. Nixon's most significant accomplishment was the detente with China that helped keep the two Communist superpowers apart during the remainder of the Cold War.

His ability to create a new basis for the Republican Party eventually foundered on Watergate but was resuscitated with Ronald Reagan. Although not originating with him, President Nixon quickly learned how guile could be used to win in American politics and began to cross into criminal behavior. What transpired under Nixon and his successors was a level of sleaziness, the small-minded grubbiness that has since become a marked feature of the Washington political scene.

The Election of 1968

The increasingly leftist rhetoric of Robert Kennedy and the peace candidacy of Eugene McCarthy led to LBJ's decision to withdraw his candidacy on March 31st for re-election in 1968. The killing of Martin Luther King at Easter 1968 unleashed another orgy of riots in the streets of the District of Columbia along with so many others that seemed to reinforce all the fears that underlay the racial divide. Then the killing of Robert Kennedy in June left Hubert Humphrey alone among the candidates for the Democratic presidential nomination. Held subject to LBJ's insistence at the Democratic Convention to maintaining the commitment to the Viet Nam policy that had failed,

Humphrey was politically isolated from his normal liberal base. The disorders on the streets of Chicago at the time of the Democratic Convention and the police response punctuated the meetings. Hubert Humphrey was finally nominated as president but of a wounded party.

During the Depression era, there had not been great demand for economic redistribution, but for the restoration of order. It was not pure racism inherent in the slogan of "law and order." It was the understandable focus to make society work according to standards. The more important impetus behind the slogan was not only pure racial divisiveness but led to the election of Gary Hatcher in Gary Indiana and Carl Stokes as black mayors of white-majority Cleveland. LBJ had been attacked for no longer being in control.

After withdrawing from the University of Minnesota to help out his family, he re-enrolled in 1937. Although living in poverty, he was particularly excited by the courses in political science. A graduate student at Louisiana State University in Baton Rouge Louisiana, his master's thesis was a commitment to the policies of the New Deal. His stay there also introduced him to the unfairness and the evil of segregation. Having brought about the combination of the Farmer-Labor Party and the Democratic Party in the 1944 presidential election, he was supported by a united labor movement for election as mayor of Minneapolis in 1945. He set up a "Fair Employment Practices Commission," as the motif for his entire future career. His future political base became the DF-L Party purged of Communist influence.

At the 1948 Democratic Convention, he reclaimed the soul of the Democratic Party to "get out of the shadow of state's rights and walk forthrightly into the bright sunshine of human rights." The passage of a strong civil rights plank in the Democratic platform strengthened the left-wing credentials of President Harry Truman in opposition to Henry Wallace's Progressive Party to help win victory in the 1948 campaign. After the passage of the civil rights plank, the Dixiecrats under J. Strom Thurmond walked out.

Figure 31 - Hubert Horatio Humphrey

Hubert Horatio Humphrey Jr, born in 1911, grew up in Doland South Dakota. A town with ca 600 inhabitants, a sign post read 1342 miles to Washington. His father was the local intellectual, a follower of William Jennings Bryan. The Depression came early and stayed long; the family lost their house as well as their money when the banks failed. Fair play and equality were the two major tenets of his upbringing. Beneath it all was a belief in the Social Gospel, the bringing of a heaven to earth, of a more just economic and political order. That Gospel was to be found in the politics of the Democratic Party in a home where Bryan's Cross of Gold speech was regularly recited.

1948 was also the year HH entered the Senate, as did Lyndon Johnson. The latter was friendly to the former, otherwise merely a pariah to his southern colleagues. When LBJ became Democratic Whip in 1951, he saw HH with his civil rights credentials as a bridge to the liberal bloc. HH had become Johnson's subordinate while also still dreaming about becoming president. Running as a poor man in

1960 for the Democratic nomination, he was beaten by Kennedy money and organization in the primaries of Wisconsin and the West Virginia.

Denied the presidency, he led in the Senate as Democratic whip in 1960. Many of his ideas that were called visionary, if not crackpot, when he had put them forth, now became the Peace Corps and the Job Corps. The test came, with LBJ the successor to Kennedy, in the Civil Rights Bill of 1964. Both HH and LBJ worked together to praise Everett Dirksen to the skies to maintain Republican support for invoking cloture. With passage, HH had earned his position as vice-president with LBJ in 1964, if not already based on LBJ's aversion to the consideration of Robert Kennedy.

The price was "complete and unswerving loyalty." It was exacted sometimes in a capricious manner throughout; moreover, it was exacted to the very end at the Democratic Convention in Chicago in 1968 and even during the election campaign. HH's defeat in 1968 was due to his loyalty to his President.; The Humphrey campaign in 1968 tried to deflect the Viet Nam issue by focusing on domestic policy and the need to safeguard the social achievements of the Great Society. The need was especially true for working class whites attracted by George Wallace's message, threatened as they were by the open housing and affirmative action thrusts of the Second Reconstruction, Further, George Wallace's "law and order" stance could be easily contrasted to the disorder on the streets of Chicago as well as the streets of the black ghettoes that had occurred under Democratic Party rule.

The Democratic vice-presidential candidate Edward Muskie, helpfully of Polish Catholic extraction, shone in contrast to Spiro Agnew paired with Nixon and Curtis Lemay of Air Force Strategic Air Command (SAC) fame paired with George Wallace of the American Independent Party. Nevertheless, Congressional candidates avoided sharing platforms and resources with HH who also had far less financing from business than the Republican Nixon. HH's promise to detach himself from LBJ's war policy was causing him to rise in the polls on the eve of the election. Nixon apparently had signaled to the South Viet Nam leader to hold off from any agreement that could help the Democrats. The election was close with George Wallace failing to achieve his goal of controlling the Electoral College results.

Figure 32 - Richard Nixon

Richard Nixon had presided over the Senate and had not been idle while doing so. He knew each of the county chairmen, the money behind each senator, the results of the latest poll. He had attended meetings of the National Security Council and was more well informed although not privy to all Eisenhower's secrets. For eight years, Nixon kept himself "ready," although highly diffident about doing so at the time of Eisenhower's heart attacks. Nixon had the biennial political role for the Republican Party. Not until 1960 was he free to express his own wished of lower taxes and deficit spending. His basic stance was that the Democrats would take the country down the road to socialism at home and soft on communism abroad.

Nixon was both most hated and feared with his campaigning style full of innuendo and slashing style. To many, he seemed insincere. His politics were the politics of division but did not try to divide the country on the basis of civil rights, anti-union or on religion in the election of 1960. When he claimed to be truly knowledgeable about Eisenhower's decisions, he was faulted by Eisenhower's faint praise. Without Eisenhower's unqualified respect, Nixon's position depended on being as close to the great man as possible.

Without any money of his own, after his defeat in 1960, Nixon was said to need to pay for his daughter's college expenses. He went to work as a lawyer for a California firm. California beckoned for a political career; it would be a stopgap until possibly running for the presidency in 1968. Having written his book on his *Six Crises,* he was now prepared to run for governor of California against Pat Brown. He felt that he would be well funded by the big names of California at the Bohemian Club, But what worked rather well nationally in 1960 did not work as well locally; there was "no mess in Sacramento for him to clean up." Riding on the coattails of 1960 and his probably stolen election in Chicago no longer worked since JFK was now immensely popular with the press as well as the country. The "Cuban missile crisis" intervened on the eve of the election of 1962 and was billed as a Kennedy victory over the Soviets. Nixon lost by 270,000 votes.

On the way home after his famous "last interview" when he was described as "telling off the press," he was already planning his future. This time, he did move to New York.

Nixon won by a hair's breadth in 1968. He had claimed that he had a secret plan to end the war in Viet Nam but did not; rather he planned to escalate it. He had won only by the formerly Democratic George Wallace votes going elsewhere. He failed to achieve control in either of the two houses of the Congress. The major change was the movement of whites in the Deep South, regardless of class, away from the Democratic Party. One of the popular books of the day was *The Emerging Republican Majority* by Kevin Phillips that expressed the Republican Party taking over the southern whites.

Richard Nixon was still the first president since Zachary Taylor in 1849 to take office without a majority in either chamber. He had won office without a clear mandate and had to govern with growing opposition to the Viet Nam War at a time when the postwar consensus on both domestic and foreign policy was breaking down. Nixon's tendency to view politics in terms of crisis and conflict made him prone to secrecy and surprise. He isolated the executive from the Congress as well as the bureaucracy to strengthen power in his own hands. In Nixon's view, getting things done by whatever means necessary would be the mark of greatness. He thought that virtue is not what lifts great leaders above others. He saw himself as the embattled presidency, surrounded by the enemies while he was alone.

He saw the opposition as the enemy of himself as the embodiment of the will of the people.

Detente

What was to continue during the Nixon Administration was the absolute Executive control over foreign policy coupled with that of his NSC Director Henry Kissinger. It is important to understand that President Nixon was indeed the strategist while Henry Kissinger was the necessary tactician. Both men were suspicious of others and of each other. President Nixon meted out abuse but sought validation in equal measure. In turn, the bullied Kissinger took out his frustrations on his staff.

During the 1950's, Kissinger attacked President Eisenhower's public avowals of "massive retaliation" as a way of response to Communist support of nationalism in the Third World. In his book called *Nuclear Weapons and Foreign Policy*, he argued for the use of "tactical" atomic weapons as one weapon in settling limited wars. During the Kennedy years of the 1960"s, he replaced this stance with a more nuanced need to rethink strategy but was not welcomed by McGeorge Bundy in the White House. His increased role in the Viet Nam negotiations under LBJ stood him in good stead to carry on in that role under President Richard Nixon.

Circumstances and great common interest in foreign policy brought President Nixon and Kissinger together. The coming together also represented a union of two outsiders who distrusted establishment liberals. In addition, they both men were cynical about people's motives that outdoing opponents required a relaxed view of scruples. The choice of William Rogers as Secretary of State assured Nixon, and Kissinger, that it would be the two of them who would be in his stead. Kissinger reorganized the NSC to create a bureaucratic organization that would replace the State Department.

Figure 33 - Henry Kisssinger

Henry (Heinz) Kisssinger was born in Furth Germany in 1923 the son of a schoolmaster. His middle-class Jewish life was severely disrupted by the rise of Hitler; the family forced to emigrate to New York in August 1938. Drafted from a accountancy program at New York's City College, he was recognized for his superior intelligence and taken under the auspices of an older German scholar Fritz Kraemer. He was encouraged to transfer to Harvard entering in the class of 1950. He majored in Government to became an acolyte of William Y. Elliot. His undergraduate thesis was outstanding, assuring him a summa. As Director of the Harvard University Summer International Seminar, he was heavily subsidized by the CIA from 1952-1969.

President Nixon prcferred to work on his own in his hideaway in the Executive Office Building. Self-indulgence or wasting time was forbidden; he would not be seen as taking time off. Bob Haldeman, a former advertising man from Los Angeles, protected him from his bad temper and kept him enclosed by a "Berlin Wall." John Erlichman was the Domestic Counselor. Also a classmate of Haldeman, they were considered his closest confidantes. John Mitchell had been his New York law partner and had arranged the negotiations for his election. Patrick Moynihan was his other Harvard professor. A former Kennedy liberal, he was head of the Urban Affairs Council, the equivalent of the National Security Council.

However, since foreign relations were most important, Nixon contemptuously considered domestic relations as "building outhouses in Peoria," his major meetings were with Kissinger whose office was now in the basem0ent of the White House. They met together nearly 200 times in the first hundred days. It was no longer useful to browbeat the Democrats for being "soft on Communism." From the beginning of his term, Nixon wanted Kissinger to start contacts with the Chinese and he wanted to leave Viet Nam "with honor." They were both aware that its was the failure to leave Viet Nam that cost LBJ the presidency. The initial approach was the "Mad Man" theory of President Nixon's actions. He was to threaten unheard of actions; he still felt it necessary to maintain American commitment to its allies.

The Vietnamization of the war was Secretary of Defenses' Laird's plan and it was succeeding by reducing the impact of the draft on American youth. President Nixon advocated the use of South Vietnamese troops to take over the war after the widely supported Viet Nam Moratorium of October 15th, 1969. Although Ho Chih Minh would die in 1969, it would not affect the North Vietnamese will to wage their anti-colonialist fight. They had fought the Japanese, the French and now the Americans for decades. They were wily, stubborn and intransigent; the Russians had little power to control their allies in North Viet Nam. The CIA was stymied throughout the war by the lack of knowledge about the aims of the North Vietnamese leadership. They were unsuccessful in infiltrating the leadership.

During the electoral campaign of 1968, Nixon had talked about some sort of plan but did not actually have any plan to get out of Viet Nam "with honor." The secret bombing of Laos and Cambodia did not succeed and any other efforts to get out of Viet Nam did not suffice. The "domino" theory was no longer viable but withdrawal did not actually occur until much later. "I will not be the first American president of the United States to lose a war;" it was becoming President Richard Nixon's war.

It was at this time that Daniel Ellsberg began to copy the Pentagon Papers as a way of forcing President Nixon to leave. Without Ellsberg's knowledge, a letter from Rand colleagues opposing the war was published in the newspapers. It provided important establishment support for the war moratorium that occurred on October 15th, 1969. The success of his "Silent Majority" speech was President Nixon's answer. He would persist in his policy with increased use of South Viet Nam troops the principal effect. The activist anti-war mobilization of November 15th, 1969 was even more effective with Peter, Paul and Mary singing their songs to some 600,000 people on the National Mall. The number of men evading the draft continued to multiply as notice of the My Lai Massacre proliferated. *Life* magazine published on December 3, 1969, a graphic set of pictures of My Lai. These were part of 300 such incidents that occurred, where "kill anything that moves" was the policy.

On April 20th, 1970, President Nixon announced the increased departure of American troops from Viet Nam. During this same time, there was an increase in the up to then secret bombing raids over Cambodia that had started as early as March 1969. Although a neutral country, American military power was not anchored by concerns about morality and international law. Congress was of course not consulted. The subsequent departure of Prince Sihanouk brought about the rise of Cambodian communist forces, quite independent of the North Vietnamese. It led to the rise of the Khmer Rouge and the eventual military incursion into that country.

The issue of its secrecy became the obsessive one, per se. The resignation of four aides to Henry Kissinger was done quietly so as to not undermine him in respect to Erlichman. Kissinger was quite concerned with his access to the president, excluding other members of the cabinet such as Secretary of State Rogers and Secretary of Defense Laird. However, the decision to invade Cambodia aroused the student movement to new heights with profound consequences at Kent State and Jackson State Universities. Nowhere was this last effort a more telling consequence of the "moral majority" stance taken by President Nixon. At Kent State, the budding Republican senator,

Governor Rhodes expressed the anger using the "law and order" motif derived from the White House.

The election of 1970 proved the basis of the Kevin Phillips analysis of the coming Republican majority. The moral majority of the former George Wallace voters would combine with the Catholic ethnics and the Sun Belt conservatives. Spiro Agnew pushed his role as vice-president in response to "the nattering nabobs of negativism" in his attack on the intellectual reporters that opposed the president. Nixon tried to pull the election by the last minute changes but only succeeded in causing a message that differed from the "message of bringing people together" that he wished to project. The Senate remained in Democratic hands.

What did succeed was the plan to build relationships with the Russians and the Chinese as the broad swath of foreign policy for which President Nixon could take personal credit. Only he, with his untarnished Cold War credits, could do what he was doing. America's power was on the wane following Viet Nam; he was unable to follow his pugnacious instincts to fight back there. There were fissures between the Russians and the Chinese that were ripening. Approaches to the Chinese and Soviets might not only influence dealings with Hanoi but, more important, improve relations with the Soviets and the Chinese to approach a balance of power. They might also give President Nixon something personal to boast about in his re-election in 1972.

In September 1970, Nixon and Kissinger responded to a request to meet with the Chinese to assure that President Nixon received the credit rather than the State Department establishment. The shift in China policy was the more fundamental one. However, in May 1971, the Russians came through with the wording for the "Strategic Arms Limitation Treaty" (SALT). Nixon was delighted that he had finally accomplished something that he could claim, free of the more compartmental thinking inherent in the State Department. Soon after, the Chinese responded with the suggestion for a visit. The secrecy that was associated with the meeting projected in February 1972 was to take place before the re-election of 1972 was in keeping with the needed planned credit. In May 1972, he visited Moscow to confer with Leonid Brezhnev, the first arms-control effort of the nuclear era.

The Election of 1972

During the course of his first term, Nixon had all but erased the American troop presence in Viet Nam from 543,000 in January 1969 to 27,000 in December 1972. The size of naval and air forces was, however, the same; President Nixon had held to the Viet Nam war so as to make it his own. It had gone on for seven years; despite the great swathes of history that Nixon seemed to have created with the Soviets and the Chinese, the Viet Nam war continued. The American death toll reached beyond 50,000; twenty-thousand on Nixon's watch. Nixon's awareness of his dire straits on the eve of the 1972 election was evidenced by his actions in January 1972. He pulled out a large reduction in America troops despite the lack of progress in the peace talks in Paris with the North Vietnamese.

South Dakotan Senator George McGovern represented those in the Congress who tried to redirect American resources toward peaceful use; for his "Food for Peace" program and to reduce the militarization of American foreign policy. Even with the breakthroughs of over all foreign policy, the Chinese, for example, had not exerted their expected effect on the North Vietnamese to negotiate an appropriate method that met Nixon's standards. By playing the game of negotiating from strength, President Nixon won overwhelmingly in the election of 1972 over George McGovern.

President Nixon was re-elected by the largest plurality ever given to a chief executive in history. Nixon squandered the opportunity to campaign for his party in Congress and, as in 1960 and 1968, Republicans gained just a few seats in the House and lost seats in the Senate. The Congress would be no friendlier and potentially more hostile than his previous Congresses despite his overwhelming electoral college victory. He had managed to delay the end of the Vietnamese War until after the election of 1972 despite the onus of having extended it for no apparent purpose with its coincident loss of life.

The impact of the Viet Nam War had already begun to have an effect on American foreign policy to redirect emphasis away from a land war in East Asia toward areas closer to American interests. These included Western Europe and Japan. Without the sea of entangling alliances created by John Foster Dulles, the so-called "Nixon

Doctrine" freed the United States from the degree to which it was constrained by these entangling alliances such as by the ties to Taiwan. "We will help only where it can make a real difference and is in our interest."

The effort to disentangle himself from the Viet Nam war had been an ongoing one. In the fall of 1968, Nixon had signaled to the South Vietnamese premier that he should fail to respond to LBJ's initiative to seek peace terms but rather wait upon the Republican terms. LBJ was furious but could not call Nixon's bluff, based upon the use of wiretaps. There is no evidence that peace talks at that time would have been successful. However, Nixon had intervened in the process to assure that peace talks could not start.

During the next year, both Nixon and Kissinger tried in several ways to be able to find an "honorable" way out of Viet Nam. The blandest action was the secret bombing of Cambodia that proceeded for several years starting in the spring of 1969. The growing anti-war movement in the United States precluded any response from Hanoi to threats of further escalation made by President Nixon. This was true despite efforts to recognize Red China and to use their good offices to affect Hanoi. However, there was already mention of the possibility that the United States would withdraw and leave the South Vietnamese to fend for themselves after "a decent interval."

In the meantime, the disaster began to extend to President Nixon's presidency. As Haldeman put it, without Viet Nam, Watergate would not have happened. The abuses that led to Watergate began with Viet Nam. In 1969, came the bombing of Cambodia. The wiretapping of White House aides followed, prompted by a leak to the *New York Times* regarding the bombing. Then came the break-in of the office of the psychiatrist of Daniel Ellsberg, the author of the Pentagon Papers dealing with Viet Nam. He had been delegated while at Rand Corporation by Secretary of Defense McNamara. When finally finished in January 1969 at the start of the Nixon Administration, that report was not welcomed by the new Secretary of Defense Mel Laird. However, a copy had been placed at the Rand Corporation that had been copied by Dan Ellsberg. It seemed to indicate that the American public had been lied to consistently in relation to the war in Viet Nam. President Nixon also explicitly approved the break into the safe at the Brookings Institution in search of Viet Nam secrets from the Kennedy and Johnson Administrations but that was rescinded. In June 1971, The *New York Times*, and then the *Washington Post*, both published excerpts from the papers copied by Ellsberg. John Mitchell then approved the break-in at the Watergate.

In the winter of 1970, Larry O'Brien had been made head of the Democratic National Committee headquartered in the Watergate Office Building. Head of JFK's campaign in 1960, President Nixon regarded O'Brien with a mixture of the apprehension and respect that he reserved for the Kennedy's and their political organization that had beaten him back then. The president is quoted by Haldeman to "move hard" on Larry O'Brien. Nixon ordered the IRS to audit the tax returns of O'Brien as well as potential Democratic front-runners. He thought that he and his friends had been so audited after his 1960 defeat.

Chuck Colson was his henchman to carry out his attacks. Colson was seen by the other Nixon intimates as "catering to [President Nixon's] worst instincts." For example, Nixon was delighted when a committee was formed to falsely associate vice-president nominee Maine Senator Muskie with support of busing.

Irked that Kissinger had been seen as the instigator rather than merely the executor of foreign policy initiatives, Nixon reinstalled the taping system to record the historical record as Nixon wished it recorded. Activated by the Secret Service, the recordings were voice-activated so as to be activated by the all-thumbs nature of the President.

In seeking information that might be damaging to LBJ in the "Pentagon Papers" dealing with material on the Viet Nam War, President Nixon ordered what was to be his first break-in. Chuck Colson dredged up E. Howard Hunt to be the person. The "Plumber's Unit" Special Investigative Unit was set up in the Executive Office Building" (EOB) Room 16 to find the leaks that were apparently ruining the presidency. Once again, the pattern had begun to firm up that was to document the line that would actually doom the presidency.

Gordon Liddy was now working out of the Committee for the Re-election of the Presidency (CREEP). With the November 1972 election approaching, resources were being poured into the effort to re-elect the presidency for a crucial second term. Nixon had declared that he would not be outspent as he had been by the Kennedy forces in 1960. Liddy was spending money like it was going out of style, lining up prostitutes to trap wayward Democrats. W.R. Haldeman signed on for another $300,000 for "intelligence gathering" and John Mitchell, the chair of CREEP failed to put an end to all the "madness."

George McGovern was the only Democrat still standing. Nixon knew he would win; only not by how much. He had started the whole madness of Watergate by being concerned about Larry O'Brien. At the same time as President Nixon was celebrating his summit in Moscow, Liddy and Hunt were meeting with their Cuban exiles to plan the last minute details of their Watergate burglary of the Democratic National Committee. President Nixon seemed bemused by the episode when there was first note of the burglary in the newspaper. He considered the spying that had been going on as standard procedure. In the experience of President Nixon and his close associates, the use of dirty tricks was a "fact of life."

By late June, the death of J. Edgar Hoover had brought a new Director to the FBI; one who could not keep its investigation "under control." Haldeman made the recommendation that the President call in the CIA to instruct the FBI to call off its investigation. When discovered on the presidential tapes, this was the "smoking gun" that caused the resignation of the president. What had been revealed was the toxic environment created by Richard Nixon that had begun to unravel. The entire litany of names and relationships began to unravel in the pages of the *Washington Post*, whose hostility was already affected by the fact that it had been attacked by the threat to their TV licenses.

The Constitutional Crisis

Out of public view, staffers from Senator Edward Kennedy's Judiciary Committee had organized an investigation on the Watergate case. North Carolina Senator Sam Ervin was designated as Chair of the "Senate Select Committee on Presidential Campaign Activities of the Election of 1972" (The Watergate Committee). Nixon did not have anyone to talk to; he did not want to find out the truth that his closest confidantes had acted as they had.

President Nixon had begun to involve himself with James Dean in the Watergate case. The connection opened with Haldeman about the break-in. The connection with the other botched break-in re the

Ellsberg files also became evident. It was at this point that President Nixon could again have saved his presidency but he did not. When asked by Dean what to do about Hunt's wish to have his silence paid for, President Nixon asked "How much does he want?" It was just one more crisis to be bluffed and battled through; to be tricked as a political problem. However, this one was criminal. He then had to fire his closest aides.

He had appointed Elliott Richardson as Attorney General as a "Mr. Clean," a friend of Senator Kennedy. Richardson, in turn, appointed Archibald Cox as Special Prosecutor. The Harvard men were coming together in full force. Alex Butterfield had testified about the existence of the taping system in the White House. First, President Nixon had believed that the tapes would protect him; and secondarily, that the Supreme Court would not require him to give them up. It was too late to "tear them out;" who would indeed light the match? Matched against the two Harvard classmates, both veterans of Justice Learned Hand, they refused to resign over the right to retain the tapes by the President. The Saturday night of October 23, 1973 goes down in history as the "Saturday Night Massacre" when the two were required to leave office.

During the remainder of 1973 and early 1974, President Nixon remained beleaguered in the White House as the Gallup polls found his support withering. The Congress was busily writing the "Joint Resolution Concerning the War Powers of the President and the Congress." The framers made the decision to go to war a reflection of the Legislature, not that of the Executive. The "Gulf of Tonkin Resolution" passed by Congress had allowed LBJ to place a large number of troops in Viet Nam. Both the House and Senate over-rode the veto of President Nixon.

The effects of the Saturday Night Massacre reverberated in the election of 1974. The review of the tapes became clearly insupportable for his continued presidency. The Republican *Chicago Tribune* called for his resignation. President Nixon had wanted to appear in charge. Instead, he sounded weal, indecisive, and far from presidential when the tapes appeared. There had been no effective presidency for nearly a year. In July, it became apparent that he would be impeached by the House and likely to be convicted by the Senate. On the 1st of August, President Nixon decided to resign.

August 8th was his last day as president. Gerald Ford had become vice-president after the forced resignation of Spiro Agnew. In September 1974, Nixon received his pardon, having acknowledged his guilt for "crimes he may have committed as president."

The Ford Succession

Gerald Ford had no idea that he would be Nixon's vice-president nor of course his successor as president. He was compared to Harry Truman who had been unknown when tapped by FDR. Ford had been selected as a middle-of the-road Republican just as Truman had been selected as such a Democrat. An Eisenhower internationalist Republican, Ford was not a Goldwater supporter in 1964. Devotion to duty and practical approach to everyday life characterized Gerald Ford.

Two of his early decisions affected his likelihood to be re-elected in 1976. The first was the selection of Nelson Rockefeller as vice-president by a Republican Party whom its most conservative wing opposed. The second was the decision to pardon President Richard Nixon.

The low price of gasoline that enabled the post-Second World War dream of the house in the suburbs was becoming more scarce as well as an expensive commodity. Its price was suddenly a matter of geopolitics following the Arab embargo of 1973. Unlike even in the depression years, when belief in the essential fairness of the system still persisted, the solutions and the theories that had been the previous guideposts no longer seemed to work.

President Ford kept Kissinger on as Secretary of State; the latter followed through with the Helsinki Accords as part of the projected detente. Gerald Ford had visited Viet Nam when a young congressman in 1953. Still under the nominal control of the French, it was not long before the Americans had replaced them against Ho Chi Minh. Congressman Ford had not opposed the policy after the Geneva Convention when the South Viet Nam had been instituted with American support. Kissinger's agreement in Paris did not end the war but only American involvement.

Figure 34 – Gerald Ford

Born in 1913, young Ford was an Eagle Scout and football hero at University of Michigan. A graduate of Yale Law School, he fought in the Navy in the Pacific. He embarked on his first campaign in 1948 and served 13 terms as a Republican from the 5th District of Michigan centered upon Grand Rapids, his last eight years as Minority Leader. His main ambition was to become House Speaker. First appointed vice-president in 1973, he became president in August 1974 after the resignation of President Richard Nixon.

The North Vietnamese continued to infiltrate the South. As Ford took on the presidency from Nixon, the legacy of Viet Nam continued to haunt him. In an unprecedented move, the entire body of the Senate Foreign Relations Committee took action. They visited the president in the White House to inform him that no further appropriations would be forthcoming. Congress withheld further funding for South Viet Nam and the North Vietnamese took over the entire country.

President Nixon had held out for peace "with honor." Not so, President Ford concluded. He had no choice. The ignominious end of the Nixon Administration with the departure of the helicopter from the lawn of The White House was mirrored in the similarly ignominious end of the American involvement of the helicopter from the roof of the American Embassy in Saigon.

The country would have to survive its bloody and embarrassing defeat in Viet Nam but would never entirely be the same. Kissinger, when interviewed on TV, admitted that we "should have viewed it more in Vietnamese terms, rather than as part of a global conspiracy." Kissinger eventually lost his job as NSC in favor of Brent Scowcroft while Nelson Rockefeller withdrew for the forthcoming election.

During his primary battle with Ronald Reagan, President Ford was forced to call upon his CIA Director George H.W. Bush, to evaluate his agency's handling of the "National Intelligence Estimate" (NIE). His predecessor as CIA Director had rejected the idea. The CIA was accused of reducing the dangers so as to be compatible with the requirements of detente. A secondary group called Team B led by Richard Pipes of Harvard and full of men in support of rearmament found the CIA estimate wanting. Of course, Team B's findings took precedence.

A group of both Democrats and conservative Republicans had gathered together to form the "Committee on the Clear and Present Danger" that defined "detente" as a forbidden word in support of Ronald Reagan for president. Kissinger's realism was to be replaced by moralist, stridency about American virtue and its duty to combat evil. This ideological approach would dominate American foreign policy and its military budget for the next generation. It led to billions of dollars for unnecessary weapons, in thousands of lives lost and to the perpetuation of a national security state that symbolizes what we are as a nation.

President Ford had become recognized as a bumbler when he seemingly denied that the Helsinki Declaration indicated no acceptance of Soviet control of Eastern Europe. Although by far the most athletic of presidents, he was seen by the newsreels as a "bumbler." He was accused of being unable to "think of two things at the same time." He was accused by Ronald Reagan as a creature of detente and narrowly won the nomination lf his party in its convention.

By the time of the election of 1976 in the year of the Bi-Centennial, the American political landscape produced no stars and the outsider

Jimmy Carter became president. The country wanted a change from Viet Nam and Watergate; it wanted a Democrat from outside Washington; a man of deep faith, modesty and hard work. Seeing the Viet Nam war as irrelevant, Carter wished to return to America's old values and resume its rightful role as the custodian of human rights. The values of each candidate were similar. Both were moderates and the election was very close. It is interesting that President Carter's most telling statement was his acceptance of President Ford's decision to pardon President Nixon for his crimes in office.

CHAPTER 6
THE CARTER PRESIDENCY 1976-1980

Introduction

Figure 35 - Jimmy Carter

Jimmy Carter asserted in his campaign speeches that he would "never tell a lie" and had not ever been a Washingtonian. Born a member of country-gentry in rural Georgia, he went to the Naval Academy and was selected to join Admiral Rickover's nuclear fleet. After his father's death, he returned to Georgia to run for state senator. Elected governor in 1970, he won by a close margin. He was recognized by Time Magazine as an exemplar of the new South when he vowed that segregation was over in Georgia. An obscure one-time governor, he became active in national Democratic politics during the election of 1974. When Ted Kennedy took himself out of the race due to family problems, Carter took advantage of the primaries to become known in 1976. Against the field of mainly more liberal Washingtonians, he stood alone as a moderate.

He walked with his wife Rosalynn almost the entire length of Pennsylvania Avenue in his inaugural parade eschewing pomp and circumstance whenever possible. President Carter continued to exemplify his campaign strategy as he took office. He brought his campaign staff almost intact into the White House. Resenting all criticism, they saw it simply as anti-Southern snobbery. With his young aide Hamilton Jordan in control, they functioned without the method of the chief-of-staff inherited from Eisenhower's use of Sherman Adams. Almost all of his other staff came from his contacts on the Rockefeller Trilateral Commission that represented large-scale business interests and the American elite.

The objections to high taxes meant that high government spending had to be reduced. There were several impediments inherent in the nature of the Congress. One characteristic was the character of each member having some pet program that he traded for support for another's pet project leading to excessive "pork." President Carter avoided meeting the political needs of the Congress exemplified by his abrupt cancellation of such water projects based on their expense. Since the New Deal, federal bureaucracies each had their "clients" interested in their own departments. These "special interests" created and supported the budgets of the departments to which they were beholden.

This process was acceptable while the economy was expanding; it was now becoming more problematic. His vetoes were supported by Republican support despite strong Democratic party criticism. His emphasis was not in advancing the social needs of the American people for health care and aid to the cities and so forth.

In the name of increasing efficiency and profits came the deregulation of natural gas and the control of airplane routes by the Civil Aeronautical Board, A more stringent anti-union stance was in the offing. The 1978 coal strike marked the eventual demise of the United Mine Workers. Federal intervention helped break the unity of the miners, forcing a settlement based on regional interests. Any labor attempt to increase the enforcement of the Wagner Act by excessive litigation by employers was also unsuccessful; even given a Democratic president and Congress. The need for only two votes was necessary to invoke cloture of a filibuster against the bill. The number of unionized workers was being reduced while concern was voiced by cabinet officers about the "role of increased business confidence." Tax breaks to business for investment were the vehicle to encourage the necessary growth despite large amounts of cash readily available.

The Carter presidency came to be viewed not as a bunch of naive outsiders newly come to Washington. His presidency had to be responsive to the crisis of American liberalism resting upon a strong presidency, an internationalist foreign policy driven by anti-Communistic containment and social reform driven by economic growth. All three had begun to founder in his time.

The success of the Iranian Revolution in February 1979 marked a clear break in the Cold War. It introduced a clear conflict against imperialism in the Middle East that continues to persist until the present. That revolution first disrupted oil production that the Saudis soon made up but the increased supply problems caused a price rise in the United States. On Christmas Eve 1979, the Russians invaded Afghanistan. In his State of the Union address in January 1980, President Carter recognized the importance of Persian Gulf oil to American interests in the Middle East. The threat by Russia was to disrupt the flow of oil by virtue of their entry into Afghanistan. It was the first time that the Soviets had ventured beyond their borders since the end of the Second World War.

Iranian revolutionaries had seized the American embassy on November 4, 1979, and taken Americans as hostages, It was an act of war. Although urged by many to act, President Carter refused to do so. When he did so, it was a failure, bringing only further embarrassment to the United States.

Competence and Compassion

Carter was considered a centrist. His twin motifs claimed throughout his campaign and his administration would be more competent while retaining its basic compassion. He founded the Department of Energy and finally the Department of Education, so long in abeyance. To many northern liberals who were part of the Washington establishment, he appeared as an intruder with no connection with them or any others in their alliances. He was depicted as an outsider by a cartoon with an outhouse on the White House lawn.

His "careerism" does not "sing;" it was without the spirit to move souls. His engineering mind-set alienated many. The had hoped that after eight years of Republicanism they could go on with the Great Society. By 1977, he reflected the faith that government regulation might solve all national problems was beginning to fade.

One of the new initiatives his campaign developed was an opening to persons with disabilities. Prominent at his campaign opening at Warm Springs Georgia, they were energized by his election. During the interval before his inauguration, many came to Washington to prepare for his presidency only to find that their well-thought out proposals were totally ignored. There were no new initiatives in the spirit of the Great Society despite the wishes of Joseph Califano, his Secretary of HEW. Carter would not have won if some of his "special Interests" such as the labor unions had not gotten out the vote or if the blacks had not voted for him in such large numbers in the South as well as the North. His focus on balancing the budget in light of unemployment was anathema to many in the Democratic Party ranks. The sense was that the long era of economic growth was coming to an end. In his inaugural address, President Carter warned that "more" was not necessarily better. There were limits to which even our great nation could do.

Bill Clinton found that President Carter sounded more like a 17th century Puritan than a 20th century Southern Baptist. His religious background was not really that of a fundamentalist; he frequently quoted the liberal theologian Paul Tillich. Yes, man has fallen. but alleviation is possible, even if perfectibility is not. Ultimately, salvation is about individual souls, albeit "sick souls." The political and attitudinal background against which the Carter presidency operated should not be used to excuse its incompetence. It should be given due weight when assessing how adequately they fulfilled their commitment to both competence and compassion.

There is a limitation in the degree to which compassion can be provided without redistribution. The problem of race relations cannot be dealt with without some redistribution; almost impossible in dealing with what is essentially a zero-sum game of multiple special interests.

The Limits of Power

Given the limits of resources post Viet Nam and the lack of support for the militarization of the Cold War, what could be accomplished by an improved moral stance in foreign policy? President Carter's support for the appointment of Paul Warnecke as head of his negotiating team on arms control reflected the growing discrepancies in the arms control establishment. Unlike Paul Nitze and others prevalent under President Reagan who favored an increase in military spending and saw the Soviets as an implacable foe, Warnecke felt that the danger of the military might being acquired was great enough and that such might lead to miscalculations that could lead to nuclear war.

President Carter expressed his approach to foreign policy in his speech at the Naval Academy in May 1978 as essentially compatible with American values. Detente was in decline. Arms control was being attacked by the Committee on the Present Danger. American policy should support democracy. In the spirit of Wilson, it was not only relevant to Americans but to others in the world. That would free us from 'the inordinate fear of Communism, which once brought us to embrace any dictator who joined us in that fear. It had led us to fight fire with fire that is better quenched with water. America stood for more than "mere financial prosperity."

Brzenzski made himself known to various Democratic primary hopefuls but found only Jimmy Carter interested in his advice. There was significant divergence between Secretary of State Vance and the more forceful and ultimately more influential National Security Advisor Brzezinski. The latter went beyond the former to be the major strategist with the ear of the president with Vance merely the implementer of the decisions made. The NSC Director emphasized the role of the Soviet Union as a megalomaniac state and the need for the use of force in that relationship during the Cold War. He also is credited with the appreciation for the internal problems facing the Soviet Union within its empire with particular emphasis on Polish nationalism, with which he remained very engaged based on his own life experience.

Figure 36 - Zbigniew Brzezinski

Zbigniew Brzezinski was born in 1926 in Warsaw the son of Polish nobility. His mother was the grandniece of Eduard Benes, the president of Czechoslovakia; his father a Polish diplomat. He was stationed in Germany from 1931 to 1935 during the Nazi era; in the Soviet Union from 1936 to 1938 during Stalin's Great Purge and in Canada as the Polish Consul General in Montreal from 1938 onwards. Young Brzezinski grew up in Montreal and received his degree at McGill including a master's degree on the role of nationalism in the Soviet Union. At Harvard, his doctorate focused on the effects of the Russian Revolution and the role of Joseph Stalin. He worked for Kennedy, Johnson and then for Humphrey in the 1968 campaign. Moving to Columbia, he founded the "Research Institute on Communist Affairs." He headed David Rockefeller's Trilateral Commission to promote cooperation among United States, Europe and Japan.

Both President Carter and Brzezinski liked each other. Both saw themselves as outsiders in the Washington establishment that enabled Brzezinski to serve to advocate his own policy preferences to "act tough." President Carter liked the irreverence and quickness of thinking that Brzezinski brought to any new subject but maintained his own counsel. Both the NSC Director and Secretary of State Vance displayed to outsiders a lack of cooperation that came to characterize President Carter's administration.

The progress to be made in the SALT talks with the Soviets carried out under Secretary of State Vance was beset with complications despite President Carter's wishes. Human rights issues intervened as well as a re-opening toward China. The latter can be credited to the thrust of the efforts by Brzezinski for Carter to act "tough" toward the Soviets. This was the general approach taken by Brzenzski to see the Soviet issue as central. He was seen to be more willing to risk war. Moreover, his focus on the importance of the dissidents in the Soviet Union took on a moralistic tone.

The downward spiral in Soviet-American relations may have led them to deal more aggressively with the problems they faced in Afghanistan. The response to the Soviet invasion of Afghanistan in December 1979 was to insure withdrawal of Soviet forces. The CIA began to supply arms to the guerrillas fighting the Russians. There was the cancellation of the grain sales after the crackdown on Solidarity and of the 1980 Olympic Games in Moscow after the invasion of Afghanistan.

President Carter sent a message to Brezhnev threatening military action if Russia goes farther in Afghanistan. These actions were seen as precipitous by our European allies who feared an abrogation of arms control and the eventual withdrawal of the SALT II Treaty from Congress. Secretary of State Vance had successfully negotiated the Panama Canal Treaty as well as the Egyptian-Israeli Peace Treaty. He finally resigned in late spring 1980 with the response to the invasion of Afghanistan all seen as a result of the "hard policy" of his NSC Director and his opposition to the military response to the Iranian hostage crisis.

The Iranian Crisis

The Shah of Iran had long been seen by his people as an American puppet. He had returned to power via an early CIA coup after the deposition of Mossadegh in 1953. Losing support among the clergy as well as the secular forces, the shah's forces had attacked a massive rally killing many hundreds. During 1978, the focus on human rights had permitted the shah to ease up on his repression. By 1979, President

Carter was once again toasting the shah as an "island of stability." The shah appointed a military leader who failed to gain the support of the masses continually energized by the clergy. Despite notice by the State Department of his fragility, President Carter was reassured by the CIA that the shah's position was secure. Secretary of State Vance wanted the shah to be more responsive to the need for reform while Brzenzski advocated a stronger military response directly with Tehran. Terminally ill with lymphoma, the shah wavered and chose to go into exile that brought him to Palm Springs in California.

The United States recognized the Khomeini government despite the fear that there would be a Communist takeover. It was unclear to what extent their regime would bring about a thoroughly theocratic state controlled by clerics. On Sunday 28th February 1979, the American Embassy was invaded and sixty American hostages were taken. Those persons associated with Khomeini interested in following diplomatic norms were gradually pushed out or executed. While Brzenzski pushed for a military response and Secretary of State Vance pushed for a response that would end up with saving the lives of the hostages. After the success of their revolution, Brzezenski saw it as a measure of American resolve while President Carter was primarily concerned about the safety of the hostages.

President Carter felt that the national integrity of the United States was at stake in this confrontation with evil and urged prayer. He withdrew from political campaigning in a gesture reminiscent of FDR during the dark days of the 1944 election. President Carter had needlessly raised the emotional tone of the Iran hostage crisis to make it even more important. TV each day raised their significance. It became a soap opera, Ultimately, it was Day Four Hundred and Forty Four before its end. President Carter had been rated as ineffectual and his nomination questioned vis-a-vis Ted Kennedy in November 1979. After the initial burst of patriotic support sufficient to reassure his nomination, his support dwindled even lower. The belated effort to free the hostages by a military assault failed due to mechanical difficulties.

President Carter had initially striven to develop "a new world order" but had given way to a new form of containment with the development of the "Rapid Deployment Force" (RDF). In his effort to meet his needs of a more moral approach to American power, his contribution to the human rights record was one of his greatest contributions. Moreover, what he established was the Carter Doctrine, the commitment to the military action that would characterize the future for the next generation in the Middle East.

What would be required was more than the containment offered by the 1947 Truman Doctrine. Even beyond that, what would be required would be bringing order to the Middle East, making the Persian Gulf into an American protectorate to safeguard the availability of oil. He nevertheless operated with knowledge of the limits of American triumphalism that marked the role of the next president who coasted to his inaugural on the day of the release of the American hostages held by Iran.

The Carter Legacy in Washington

The long-awaited recognition of the Department of Education required its divestment from the earlier Department of Health, Education and Welfare (DHEW). Much the smallest of the federal departments, it originated from the short-lived department established during the aftermath of the Civil War but was soon relegated to the Office of Education. It then became an obscure division of the Department of the Interior and then in 1939 a portion of the Federal Security Agency. The latter was upgraded to cabinet status in 1953 as the Department of Health, Education and Welfare. Fiercely opposed by the Republican Party, the Departmental functions established by President Carter were in turn curtailed by President Reagan.

In the latter's campaign, Ronald Reagan threatened to abolish its existence as part of the opposition to federal intrusion in the decentralized nature of American education but actually failed to do so. For example, he opposed bi-lingual education and further federal intrusion in education. The Departmental building on Independence Avenue with the schoolhouse in front was named for President Lyndon Johnson.

One of the newest areas of cabinet concern was the Department of Energy that dates its origin from the Manhattan Project in 1942 to develop the atomic bomb. Transferred to the Atomic Energy Commission in 1946, in 1974 the Nuclear Regulatory Commission was responsible for regulating the nuclear power industry while the Energy

Research Development Commission was given the responsibility for the development of nuclear power for military uses. The 1973 oil embargo brought higher energy prices and its availability to the fore.

Under President Carter, the new department was established with James Schlesinger the first secretary. Its headquarters is in the James Forrestal Building adjacent to L'Enfant Plaza on Independence Avenue.

The United States Holocaust Memorial and Museum

Figure 37 - The United States Holocaust Memorial and Museum

In 1978, almost a full generation following the end of the Second World War, President Carter created a Presidential Commission on the Holocaust that recommended a National Holocaust Memorial. The timing was related to the 30th anniversary of the State of Israel and a visit to Washington of the then Prime Minister Menachem Begin as well as even more narrow political issues. Stuart Eizenstat, from Atlanta, was the key person in the White House. The Commission made a deliberate decision to place the Memorial in a larger American context by building a museum with an educational mission. By functioning under governmental auspices, a process was initiated that led to some degree of universinality of the event. It became necessary to recognize not only the history of the Jews but of other victims of the war and, potentially of other past and future genocides. The language used by Elie Weisel, the chair of the Commission, sought to protect the uniqueness of the Holocaust: "All Jews were victims but not all victims were Jews."

There were constant battles about the membership of the Holocaust Memorial Council that replaced the Commission that was responsible for the implementation of the Report. Concern was always that the central Judaic core of the Holocaust would be obscured. In 1979, there was also the beginning of the annual ceremonies commemorating the Jewish Holocaust, but also of others, in the Capitol Rotunda in Washington. Again, in entering the larger political arena, there is the struggle to maintain the integrity of the Jewish memory in a sea of contradictions. Particularly problematic in the Museum as well as Memorial ceremonies are the claims of ethnic Poles and Ukrainians for recognition, given the anti-Semitism that imbued their nationalism and their roles during the Holocaust.

In the Americanization of the Holocaust, in the American public schools, the teaching was related to our national values. It was taught that the Holocaust was an example of the abrogation of the principles of pluralism, respect for differences and freedom from prejudice

Opened in 1993, it stands adjacent to the Mall and within sight of the Washington Monument. It has taken its place in the itinerary alongside the other museums and monuments of the busloads of high school students and families visiting Washington from all over the country, the majority non-Jewish. For those who come, there is " a new recognition of the tenets of American Constitutional democracy: a belief in equality and equal justice under law, a commitment to pluralism and tolerance ...For American Jews, it is a place of pilgrimage and a source of pride...it represents the arrival of the American Jewish community as confident and self-assertive." A generation ago, the museum would have been built in New York, not in Washington, the Jewish community would then have preferred to keep their bereaved memories private, parochial. A generation ago, Jews had internalized the rule of emancipation "be a Jew in your house, but be a man in the street." Now, in pluralistic America, the most painful of Jewish memories can be brought to the center of American life.

CHAPTER 7
THE REAGAN PRESIDENCY 1980-1988

Introduction

President Carter had spoken of limits and "malaise," As we passed through a litany of anniversaries in the 1970's, it became harder to view our country as something new; we had become the recipients of the oldest written constitution governing any country. Moreover, President Carter had failed to act to lower unemployment in tune with the quadrennial electoral cycle that had served previous presidents so well.

The election of what was to be our oldest president thus far seemed to rejuvenate America. He did not appear old. Ronald Reagan was an icon but not like Norma Desmond of *Sunset Boulevard*. He does not argue for American values; he embodies them by virtue of the continuity of his long life and his appearance. He was our "movie."

The issue of the Panama Canal had been in the forefront during the Carter Administration. Ronald Reagan had been the spokesperson of the conservative strand of the Republican Party in the primaries in his fight with President Ford in 1976. The Treaty squeaked through by a single vote under the auspices of President Carter. The results tended to affect the political scene for the next two elections. The Democratic Party was weakened by the defeat of Franck Church of Idaho and George McGovern of South Dakota but also the loss of Birch Bayh to Dan Qualye in Indiana. But, so was the loss of moderate Republicans like Clifford Case of New Jersey and Jacob Javits of New York. The latter was replaced by the Republican Alphonse D'Amato of Long Island.

The election of 1980 marked the greatest repudiation of an American president with Ronald Reagan earning 51%, John Anderson 7%, and President Carter only 41% of the vote. President Carter had entered the election cycle with inflation running into two figures, an impossible situation for re-election. The Republicans gained control of the Senate for the first time since 1954. The Democrats retained control of the House with Tip O'Neill as Speaker. Although he looked like an old Democratic Party boss, O'Neill adapted to the new ways and mastered them.

The Democrats won relatively few elections based on income redistribution in the 1980s, while the Republicans won relatively many based on cultural values. The Republican Party traded on its apparent adherence to traditional American values in opposition to abortion and same-sex marriage while the military budgets bulged and deficit spending rose. The DOD budget had ranged around $350 billion (in constant 2015 dollars) throughout the 1970's. During the Reagan Administration, it ranged as his as $550 billion in 1985 before falling to $500 billion in 1988.

The Democrats did even better in 1982, particularly in California where, by redistricting the Democrats elected 28 representatives over the 22 elected in 1980. In 1984, the "Moral Majority" was out in full force. The Religious Right wished to get the government off the back of American voters but also to insert God into the classroom. The government would become central to the business of God while capitalism was also in ascension.

Soviet-American relations in the late 1960's and early 1970's were much less volatile than earlier. With each superpower commanding approximately the same nuclear capability to destroy each other, the risks of escalation remained even greater than before because of an accident. Detente was turning a dangerous situation into a more predictable one, with a view to maintaining the post-1945 geopolitical settlement as well as for humanity at large. The centerpiece of detente was Soviet-American effort to limit the nuclear arms race. The SALT talks, initiated during the Nixon Administration, represented acknowledgement on the part of the United States that Mutually Assured Destruction; that remaining defenseless against a nuclear attack was the best way to prevent one from happening. SALT II was much less successful. It had been withdrawn from consideration by President Carter when passage could not be assured.

Figure 38 - Ronald Reagan

Ronald Reagan was born in 1911; his father a storyteller and alcoholic. They finally settled in Dixon Illinois, a town of ten thousand. The father was Irish Catholic; the mother a member of the Disciples of Christ with whom young Reagan identified. Participating in school plays gave him the satisfaction he lacked for his poor ability in sports. He went to the religiously based tiny Eureka College, graduating in 1932. He worked as a radio announcer on his way to Hollywood. At Warner Brothers, he rose in a series of relatively successful but not spectacular pictures. The head of the Screen Actors Guild, Reagan sided with the movie producers in favor of the House Un-American Activities Committee. His reputation as an anti-Communist became the basis for his politics. Employed by General Electric, he became skillful in expressing the principles that he demonstrated starting during the 1964 Goldwater campaign.

It was no source of strength for the Soviet Union to be sustaining a defense burden that was three times that of the United States GDP by an economy that was one-sixth the size. Although nuclear dangers were diminished, the credibility of their demand economy was diminishing; it became harder to defend that the few powerful leaders had the right to determine how everyone else lived. The Soviet support for Marxist efforts in Angola in Africa; its invasion of Afghanistan led to an increase in the price of their oil that mitigated against a more fundamental reorganization of the Soviet economy. People's movements in both the satellite states and in Russia itself also began to arise. Pope John Paul II in Poland; Deng Xiaoping in China questioned socialism there. From California, a broadcaster turned actor and politician could see that detente had been meant to perpetuate the Cold War; that only killing detente could end by killing the Cold War.

After the defeat of President Ford in 1976 by President Carter, Ronald Reagan was the favored son of American conservatism. Enhanced by his role as governor of California in opposition to student protests, he was the Republican candidate in 1980. His claim that the government could not be trusted became the truism of American politics. He described the federal bureaucracy as ineffective. Government might be failing but America was not. They were part of a divine plan for this great country between the oceans to be settled by those possessed of "an abiding sense of freedom and a special kind of courage." Reagan ran against George H.W. Bush in the primaries. Once Bush had agreed to oppose abortion despite his long held support for it, the Reagan-Bush ticket took shape. It was fortified by the activist Heritage Foundation funded by the beer baron Joseph Coors and Richard Mellon Scaife. The campaign was also supported by the evangelicals of the "Moral Majority" who were experiencing the breakdown of the family and the sense of social disorder.

Hollywood on the Potomac

January 20, 1981 was the start of the decade that changed America. Not since the inauguration of Andrew Jackson when the muddy boots of the mobs trampled the White House had the national capital witnessed such a spectacle. It was an outpouring of wealth and privilege. The airport could not accommodate the outpouring of private jets. So brisk was the limousine business that that calls went out as far south as Atlanta and as far north as New York City. The catering business was at full force while mink furs inundated hotel coat racks. It was the costliest, most opulent inauguration thus far in American history. Johnny Carson quipped: "This is the first administration to have a Hollywood premiere. "

Its star was a Hollywood figure who represented the cocky but unassuming figure, the American nice-guy next door with his humor and informality as well as patriotism. He was his own best speech writer; he had been the best creator of his image and his own best messenger. His role as an actor, union president, PR man for GE, and his own good fortune, had made him sure of a happy landing. With some faith, like his early 1940's movies, virtue would triumph. It was clear that the part he played was what he was; one could not separate the part from reality. Although born in the Mid-West, his pioneer credential was that of California; in being liked, in being eminent, in his lack of concern for earned credentials. His impulse was to govern *against* the government. He too was as an outsider in Washington.

The previous years had seen the loss of confidence that had marked America at the end of Second World War. Its success in 1945 had reached its culmination with the arrival of President Kennedy on the national scene in the 1960's. JFK had been murdered; LBJ had been deposed by his failure in Viet Nam; Nixon had been deposed after Watergate. Ford had been selected without ever having been elected; Carter had gone down in ignominy because of the Iran hostages. Both Martin Luther King and Malcolm X had been assassinated; Robert Kennedy and George Wallace on both wings of the Democratic Party had been removed. An already strong cynicism was reinforced; vitality of the political process was numbed.

In the decades up to 1980, it had been clear that United States was exceptional. Ever since 1914, its strength had been recognized as a model for the world. One of the themes that the candidate Ronald Reagan expounded was that of the role of the United States as an "exemplar" nation. By that, he meant not only as it was for many millions of immigrants and even would-be immigrants. Drawing upon the model expressed by John Winthrop for his exclusionist Puritan Commonwealth, President Reagan believed that it is within our preordained destiny to show all mankind that they too can be free even not left from their native share.

America's role was also for some a "redeemer" nation to illustrate the role of liberty and freedom for the world to see. Redeemers are not necessarily proactive to redeem their role, they just need to exemplify it for others to choose to follow. To what extent did President Reagan actually believe this? Many of the Founding Fathers at the end of the 18th century voiced their role as a people chosen by God for a special mission in a divine plan. For even Tom Paine as well as John Adams, the settlement of America was the opening of a grand scene in Providence, for the illumination of the ignorant and the emancipation of the slavish part of humanity all over the earth. General George Washington saw the hand of Providence in providing the support of the French Alliance toward the successful completion of the Revolutionary War. In the Federalist papers, James Madison once again called the hand of Providence to have manifested itself.

The Protestant religion in America confirmed that same sense as their belief to be successors to Israel as God's chosen people. Among them was a special calling to be righteous and an exemplar to the nations. America was deemed analogous to ancient Israel with Deuteronomy highly quoted in the political discourse of the time. Some even found support for the republican model in the Hebrew Commonwealth founded by Moses. This faith-based rhetoric and conception of American national identity had at its core a set of values that American power and ingenuity would make for a better world for all people. This belief continued to resonate with, motivate and inspire President Ronald Reagan in his own time.

Despite this understanding of the divine origins of the republic, for many, America is exceptionally prone to delusion about its own innocence as history's political messiah. It has been America's peculiar vision of national pride to clothe itself with a purity of motive and preset itself as a new beginning for mankind. The sense of America as mankind's "last best hope" as expressed by President Lincoln at Gettysburg, whose fulfillment is claimed to be found in liberty, or equality or individual rights. It can also blind a nation to the finiteness of its vision and the limits of its power. The dangers of this vision have been limited by the fact that this view is not held universally by all

Americans nor has American power been so concentrated as to exert unlimited power over others.

Supply Side Economics

The conjunction of cumulative disenchantment with Washington policies, the arrival of President Ronald Reagan and the re-emergence of laissez-faire as the operative philosophy all contributed. Indicative of the administration's policy was its selection of Raymond Donovan as Labor Secretary. Charged with "developing the welfare of wage-earners," he had been a partner in a large-scale construction firm. His confirmation was held up for multiple infractions by his company under OSHA on work-place safety as well as the corruption of Teamster officials to guarantee labor peace. Another of President Reagan's most salient early accomplishments was his action in the Professional Air Traffic Controllers strike in 1981. The firing of the strikers with significant effects on air safety determined the direction of his labor policy.

President Reagan's advisors counseled him to devote his energies to the prime task of his domestic policies. He was in no hurry to deal with issues of foreign policy he knew little about. He disregarded all the accumulated wisdom of using his political capital to draw dividends down the road. He did not see his immediate role in dealing with the agenda of the hard right regarding prayer in the schools or abortion. He sought to deal with the inflation that had plagued President Carter. It was that had led to the latter's defeat. President Reagan's first action was to cancel the embargo on sales of grain to the Soviets put in place to punish the Slviets for their incursion into Afghanistan.

One of the principles by which President Reagan came to the presidency was by adhering to the Republican Party philosophy of "supply-side" economics. Nothing had appeared on the national scene since the early New Dealers, filled with ideas for remaking the American system. No less imbued with their ideas than their predecessors of the 1930's, the conservative theorists of the 1980's were determined to undo the modern welfare state created by the New Deal and replace it with a new model.

Supply-siders were the descendants of the tax-cut revolution that flowered in California and the heirs of the candidate Ronald Reagan "get the government off our backs." Cut tax rates at the highest margins and miracles would occur. Lowering the higher margins of tax rates would lead persons to work harder, tax income would then increase by encouraging harder work by those who are productive. Unlike the poor, the investments of the rich flow into banks to stimulate further investments, if not just tax shelters. They would then also encourage persons operating outside the tax system to find their activity in so doing less likely. Lowered tax rates and reduced government regulation would permit business to thrive. By increased production, there would be lowered prices and increased number of jobs. Since taxes had reached a point where they drained the economy, tax cuts would pay for themselves. The "Laffer Curve" could be used to illustrate this principle of the effect of lowering tax rates.

For too long, according to the supply-siders, Washington policy makers had been dominated by the "demand model", that consumer purchasing power drives the economy. For too long, Washington followed the model of John Maynard Keynes who sought to control the ups and downs of the economic cycle by priming the pump of government spending when consumer spending lagged or of the monetarists from the Federal Reserve who sought to increase the money supply. All this could enable the Republicans to increase military spending without causing a budgetary deficit. Following the direction already marked by President Carter, non-military spending could also be reduced by cutting "waste" and depriving those dependent on such spending, albeit only for their own ultimate benefit.

This concept of supply-side economics proposed to free business with the opportunity to experience the first tax rate as low as that provided by Calvin Coolidge in 1924. The effect was to raise the amount of income distribution to the rich. The Gramm-Latta Act was passed in 1981 with a large number of Democratic "boll-weevil" votes in the House. This occurred in the midst of the national euphoria after President Reagan's recovery from the attempted assassination. Several Republicans including Senator Robert Dole, chair of the Budget Committee, voted against. He found the arithmetic did not quite add up. All the high sounding rhetoric covered up the real secret to which David Stockman was cognizant. It was expected that budget deficits of one hundred billion dollars in social programs would be necessary to encompass the increases in military spending and to offset the tax reductions.

Figure 39 - David Stockman

David Stockman was born in southwest Michigan, the eldest son of Republican fruit farmers. Goldwater was his hero. He studied history at Michigan State and then theology at Harvard Divinity School. Sponsored by Daniel Patrick Moynihan from Harvard, he came to Washington to become Director of the Republican Conference for whom he wrote an article deprecating all social welfare programs. He was able to run for office from his conservative home district. While in the House, he acquired a reputation for attacking public programs. Under the auspices of Republican Senator Jack Kemp, he was appointed head of the Office of Management and Budget (OMB). He frenetically cut social programs while retaining subsidies for business while the Laffer Curve was to cut in as his cuts in taxes took effect.

Casper Weinberger had been a California associate of Reagan as state finance director and then Budget Director and then Secretary of HEW under President Nixon. In both these positions, he had impounded funds rather than have them directed for social programs. Now secretary of defense, the largest of government agencies,

Weinberger faced off Stockman. He approved nearly every request for arms and every gold-plated delivery system that came across his desk. In his inaugural address, President Reagan faced west; he faced Arlington National Cemetery. In his peroration, he invoked the martial arts that had motivated the men buried there. Beginning in 1981, the U.S. Army began spending its advertising dollars on high testosterone ads; selling its recruits with its new message "we need you in the Army." It is the place to be. The Congress passed his initial army request for a 20% increase in the first year's budget of the Pentagon with the promise to double its budget in five years.

Budget deficits piled up; the Treasury found a reason to accept the large deficit as less disruptive than reducing the spending in light of Democratic Party opposition. Stockman, in an interview for the *Atlantic Monthly*, in December 1981 admitted the supply-side economics was merely another example of "trickle-down" economics that favor the rich. It was, in fact, a method for starving social welfare programs.

President Reagan was forced to raise taxes despite his faith in the essential value of the Laffer Curve, despite all the evidence to the contrary that was piling up. The national debt had risen in his first four years as had been accumulated in our national history to that point. The unemployment rate had risen to over 10%. Overall, President Reagan ultimately delivered lower taxes and somewhat less government regulation of business; and generally left decisions to individuals and markets. The price paid for the high inflation induced by President Reagan was the old story after every recession, his unemployment that hurt the poor more than the rich. His belief that social programs caused little change caused the erosion of the requests for social programs to occur.

In the decade ending in 1987, the average income of the lowest 10% fell 10% to $3157. The average of the top 10% rose some 24% to $89, 743. The average of the top 1% rose to just over $300,000, a whopping 74% increase. Affluent Americans were thronging the Hampton, Gold Coast Florida, and Palm Desert California. Unprecedented disposable income brought them there. The average wage of the white male factory worker fell; their jobs no longer existed. The cultural and economic markers to lead to middle class life and a chance for the kids to go to college had disappeared. Caste and class constraints that had begun to ease after the Second World War had begun to re-emerge. The poor ceased to vote in large enough number.

Reaganomics did have a constituency; the top 10% were doing well and the 10% below were holding their own. The actual ballot-pulling electorate was low enough to give the Republican middle class their pluralities.

The Course of the Cold War

The atomic bomb was never used during the Cold War between 1947 and 1991. After the detonation in the summer of 1945 over Hiroshima and Nagasaki, the Soviets exploded their first atomic bomb in the summer of 1949 at a desert site in Kazakhstan. President Truman was astounded that "those Asiatics" had built a nuclear weapon and Stalin was astounded at how quickly it had been detected by picking up the fall out.

In 1945, American power was at its height as the greatest power in all history. Despite the trillions of dollars subsequently spent on the military and its frequent engagements, the United States has not won a decisive military victory since. What the United States got was a national security state with a permanent war economy maintained by a military-industrial complex, not unlike that of the Soviet Union. The United States had far greater resources than the Soviet Union to sustain this effort but did not have the resources to deal with its other needs in education and in redressing its other needs.

The original impulse had been to make nuclear technology freely available. That initial impulse began to conflict with the existence of Soviet bombs and atomic spies. Klaus Fuchs had been the Russian spy who had transmitted the information to the Soviets, even with respect to the H-bomb. The Rosenberg trial ended with their death sentence in the fall of 1953. In June 1953 Wisconsin Senator Joseph McCarthy exerted his influence to create the sense of fear of spies infiltrating the government.

The decision was made by President Truman to go ahead with the development of the H-bomb in January 1950 while announcing it would never be used in war. At Lawrence-Livermore Laboratories, Edward Teller pursued the idea of the super bomb and demonstrated it at Eniwetok Island on the eve of the election of 1952. Andrei

Sakharov was the Soviet counterpart of Edward Teller; the Soviets too created the super bomb to harness fusion. The Russians found their own super bomb in 1955.

The question remained unanswerable. To what extent was an atomic weapon useable in war? To President Truman and other future presidents, there was no war that could be ultimately acceptable that would destroy civilization. That same tone was heard in speeches by Soviet leaders. Eisenhower's response, although he was the least of the war mongering persons, in his State of the Union address in January 1958. spoke of "truth, honor, justice, liberty for all...how are we to preserve them when we are opposed by people who scorn them."

The level of American terror rose in face of the Soviets waging total cold war. In August 1957, the Soviets launched their first ICBM and on October 4th, 1958 they launched Sputnik; it was all a bluff. There were but six missiles and those would take 20 hours to make operational. The famed American "missile gap" did not exist but the terror rose still higher.

In the United States, a master plan was first drafted in 1960. President Eisenhower determined it to be "overkill." President Kennedy was also uneasy with the concept of "massive retaliation" but his 1962 plan was that of "counterforce." The aim was to direct force to the missiles rather than population centers. Would not the counterforce have to be directed first rather than await an attack? Rather, they called for "mutual assured destruction" (MAD) needed to destroy up to 25% of the Soviet population and up to 50% of its industrial base. The number of Minuteman missiles was capped at 1000; 41 Polaris submarines and 500 strategic bombers would form the arsenal for MAD. Both Kennedy and Khrushchev exercised restraint in the Cuban Missile Crisis of October 1962. Khrushchev too had been bluffing.

Over decades, the dangers intensified as the weapons were invented and reinvented to carry enormous destructive power, enhanced by ever faster delivery, super accuracy and invulnerability. For the first time in history, the use of nuclear bombs offered the possibility of destroying a country before one has defeated or even engaged its armed forces. After a half-century, the warhead on a missile could be delivered across oceans in thirty minutes. No matter how many bombs nor how powerful they were, the military in both countries needed more; and those too had to be more powerful. By the end of the 1950's, the 400 atomic bombs had proliferated to 7000; by 1967 to 32,000. Three hundred bombs would destroy civilization, yet no president asked the Pentagon why it would need so many. With the invention of nuclear weapons, politicians suddenly realized that war would not lead to victory; that both sides would lose.

The Soviets finally reached parity in the early 1970's; thinking began to change. Instead of preparing pre-emptive strikes, they moved toward a posture for assured retaliation, of a "second strike." At this time, there was the first of the strategic arms control negotiations and detente blossomed. The Soviet build-up was driven by its defense industrialists as the group of aging leaders carried on under the seriously ill Brezhnev. All three missile systems were proposed and implemented, at great cost to the Russian people. In the 1970's, the United States began to deploy a Minuteman III missile that contained three warheads called the "Multiple Entry-independently Targetable Re-entry Vehicle" (MIRV). The Soviets matched and surpassed this technology, deploying their SS-18 that could carry a payload seven to eight times that American MIRV.

On entry into office in 1969, President Nixon was briefed on his war plan. There were three options presented to him: "Alpha" for strikes on primary military targets; "Bravo" for attacks on secondary industrial targets; "Charlie" for attacks on industrial population centers. Nixon was overwhelmed by the millions of deaths predicted. The Soviet leaders were also overwhelmed. Nixon called for the cessation of production of biological weapons and the Soviets signed the treaty in 1972 to go into force by 1975 but nevertheless still covertly carried on their own development.

In the late 1970's with SALT I in effect merely limiting the number of launch pads, a group of American defense policy conservatives formed the "Committee on the Present Danger" to warn of continued Soviet efforts to assure their superiority. They questioned the policy of detente pursued by President Nixon that led to SALT I. One of whose board members was Ronald Reagan, then a candidate for office. His supporters included a base of support among the social, economic and defense conservatives who opposed the SALT II Treaty then awaiting approval in Congress.

In 1976, the CIA and an outside group set up a debate questioning the goals of the Soviets while also questioning their capabilities. The CIA group questioned the likelihood of Soviet capabilities offered by the other team made up of civilian consultants. In the summer of 1980, President Carter, then facing an election campaign against Ronald Reagan, raised the military budget, specifically targeting the Soviet political leadership. By 1982, the combined strategic arsenals of the superpowers held the explosive power of one million Hiroshima's. In 1984, the Soviet leaders, fearful of their being destroyed before they could retaliate, built what could be called a "Doomsday Machine" to act in the absence of their official orders.

Not since the early days of the Cold War did President Ronald Reagan so successively sound the alarm about the Soviet Union menacing the world. Iran was menacing the Middle East; Hanoi had conquered all of Indo China; Castro was trying to turn the Caribbean into "a red sea." He felt that arms control was not the answer; the Soviets could not be trusted. President Reagan persisted in the Manichean description of an "evil" empire and continued to increase the military budget. His first military budget rose $30 billion over that of President Carter. By 1984, it had risen 60% higher military budget by the end of his first four years in office.

Nuclear balance defined the Cold War and would continue to define it forever. In the midst of this heightened military build-up, At the same time President Reagan spoke to the National Society of Evangelicals of the "evil empire," In the same period, the president was countering popular agitation for a nuclear freeze. President Reagan announced two weeks later in March 1983 the beginning of a defensive system designed to overcome in space the missiles aimed at the United States. He also spoke of sharing this technology with the Soviets. Dismissed in Washington, let alone Moscow, it was designated in the press as a "Star Wars" fantasy.

It was the perfect story of President Reagan as a storyteller; it had great popular appeal. Its origins remain obscure. One less likely theory is that his recognition came about after his visit to North American Aerospace Defense Command (NORAD). Another placed it in his experience with space films in the 1940's. Still another placed it in his fantasies in which the scientists who had placed the world in the shadow of the nuclear bomb might now create for America and the world a new science acting in the guise of American exceptionalism.

At the same time, the Pershing II missile being installed in western Europe, It was particularly fearsome to the Soviet leaders for its direct threat to them in Moscow. It led them to see the possibility of a threat that was totally highly unlikely. There were no plans to attack Moscow. In their own paranoid state, there was the real danger of a possible nuclear holocaust.

Plans for strategic defense had been continued encouraged by no less than Edward Teller of H-bomb fame. President Reagan did not wish to base his defense on mutual vulnerability. Despite the wishes of the arms control establishment, the president wished to go beyond the aims of SALT II. He advocated START, (The Strategic Arms Reduction Treaty). There were already thirty thousand nuclear weapons. The SALT treaties merely reduced the rate of growth. There were no defenses against incoming missiles; under the doctrine of MAD, to have been had been a good thing.

President Reagan was completely convinced of the SDI as his answer - to protect our people; not merely avenge them. It gave him a way to avoid the pitfalls of the nuclear "freeze movement" in the short run. In his "Star Wars" speech, President Reagan laid it out as though easily done in his March 1983 announcement. All these factors pointed toward his advocacy of the "Strategic Defense Initiative" (SDI) that made him a nuclear abolitionist. SDI was finally was announced in March 1985 with a budget of twenty-five billion. This was at a rate twice that of the Manhattan Project that had produced the atomic bomb in the 1940's. Mainstream scientific organizations such as the Union of Concerned Scientists and the American Physical Society declared the project impractical as a defensive shield. In actuality, there were fundamental problems with the defensive capabilities of the SDI. The Russians could certainly mount programs to counter it. The Soviets could mount many hundreds of decoys with their warheads, multiplying the number of targets that the SDI would need to deal with.

What had happened in the meantime was a far more relaxed relationship via Ambassador Dobrynin and Secretary of State Shultz and the advent of the more reformist Andropov as successor to Leonid Brezhnev. By August 1983, discussions had occurred based on these contacts. But then, the downing of the Korean Airlines plane and a belligerent statement by Andropov once again clouded the atmosphere. An exercise in December 1983 with NATO allies involved command and control procedures with nuclear weapons. The Soviets had always suspected that an attack would take place under such circumstances. Able Archer 83 was construed to be such and was taken seriously in Moscow. Pershing II missiles were approved by the West German Parliament and were being installed in Germany at the same time.

The victory in the 1984 election against Walter Mondale colored by TV ads proclaiming "America is Back!" had also occurred that freed President Reagan's hand to pursue his efforts for arms control in association with Secretary of State Schultz. It was consistent with President Reagan's personality; it was a "nice weapons" system; it was defensive, it killed missiles not people. For the first time, we have thought not of *offense* based on the threat of counter attack with surviving forces because there has been no alternative. For the first time, there might be a way to *defend* against an attack and rely less on nuclear weapons. They were mere dreams, and those were actually classified. Although actually far off, it seemed to be in the capability of the superior American computer skills to achieve that level of capability far sooner than the Soviets, if ever.

Now space was being opened for later investors. Any progress in space will be credited to American technology and capitalism as well as national pride. It was not entirely incidental that a large majority of prime space contracts went to California firms and to the districts of members of the Armed Services Committees in Congress. Both the Department of Defense and that of State had their own conflicting purposes in pushing through the "research" program for the SDI. Defense backed it for its protection of missile sites; State for its value in disarmament talks. Neither could predict it to serve to protect the population sufficiently with its less than perfect accuracy. But the public joined with the president in their faith that scientists would come through. It was, after all, an American faith.

President Reagan had simultaneously increased military spending. There could be no equality of effort that equated the 15% of Soviet GNP that was being expended to the six times as large American economy. It was also President Reagan's self-confidence; that communism could not succeed against capitalism based on the evidence of its failure to have done so. Yuri Andropov, former head of the KGB, died after suffering from chronic kidney disease, His successor was Cherenkov, suffering from emphysema. After the relatively long reigns of Stalin, Khrushchev, and Brezhnev, in the past several years, there had been three Soviet leaders. Sponsored by Yuri Andropov, Michael Gorbachev had now come to the fore.

Margaret Thatcher had met Gorbachev and had been impressed by him; she made her experience with him known to her friend President Reagan. In January 1985, President Reagan in his State of the Union Address saw that detente had granted the Soviets legitimacy as equal to the United States in its ideology. At the end of his address, he spoke directly in his own words to the Russian people. The image was that of two gunslingers standing permanently armed facing each other. Detente had been designed to perpetuate the Cold War; stability had been the goal. Tempered by his own early religious training, President Reagan feared that an accidental firing might set off an "Armageddon." What if the Soviets had lost what was its ideological appeal? For example, the Polish workers in "Solidarity" no longer saw it as the wave of the future.

In November 1986, President Reagan recognized in the newly appointed Gorbachev a man who recognized that things in the Soviet Union might be different. The president had long wished to meet the Soviet leader "man to man." In their first summit in Geneva in December 1985, they agreed to dismantle nuclear arms. The two forged a testy bond and their subsequent correspondence reflected a more mutual relationship. At the apogee of his presidency, budget cuts had to be considered, and reducing the military budget were in the offing. Arms control had to be part of his package; his popularity in the polls reflected that stance.

In January 1986, Gorbachev suggested an elimination of all nuclear weapons by 2000. To the consternation of Secretary of Defense Weinberger and CIA Director Casey, President Reagan's response was why wait until then. At the 27th Congress of the Russian Communist Party in late February, Gorbachev had outlined the need to work together with the United States as part of an interdependent world. The decision to leave Afghanistan was also made in this context. This may have marked the move to end the Cold War but was not fully recognized in Washington. In the ideological nature of the Reagan Administration, Gorbachev was generally seen as pursuing an aggressive strategy. Secretary of Defense Weinberger was still calling for the usual Cold War response to Soviet aims.

They agreed to a proposal to eliminate all ballistic missiles. The nuclear accident at Chernobyl in April 1986 and the lowered price of oil on the world market forced Gorbachev's hand. He called for in September 1986 a meeting that took place in November in Iceland.

Ill-prepared and ill-conceived, the summit had apparently led to an agreement to follow with a draft treaty for implementation of arms reduction. There were to be drastic reductions in strategic and medium range missiles. The Americans were unprepared for the concessions the Soviets were prepared to make. It had been assumed to be merely a "base camp" in preparation for a later summit. On the advice of Richard Perle, a leader in the re-armament camp, President Reagan turned down the Soviet offer to continue the SDI on a research basis alone. The planned draft treaty failed; President Reagan refused to give up his commitment to the SDI. The 1986 election had elected both a Democratic House and Senate. There was little time left for him to implement his dream of a nuclear reduction.

The entire arms control team were flabbergasted. What had the president bargained away? Brent Scowcroft among others was among those who thought President Reagan proposal at Reykjavik Iceland "insane." Yet if the summit had not failed on the basis of the SDI, it would have been a "disaster." Scowcroft thought the president's proposal for the SDI a wild fantasy. He believed that the national security apparatus had failed to compensate for the president's inadequacy and romanticism.

The direction taken had clearly been based on the initiative of the president; he had urged the all-night sessions that had occurred in preparation for the last final day. The pesident cherished two fantasies. One was that one could abolish nuclear weapons. The other was to replace them with an "impregnable" shield. There were other countries that had nuclear weapons at that time including China, Great Britain, France and Israel. They were unlikely to adhere to giving up their own nuclear weapons or that the U.S. Congress would agree to such a treaty at that time.

The SDI was clearly unlikely; yet the threat of it in the hands of the Americans president seemed to be a major factor to Gorbachev. President Reagan got Gorbachev to agree to its feasibility by believing so fervently in it himself. The refusal of President Reagan's to give up his dream of the SDI caused Gorbachev to accept its feasibility. He recognized that the Soviet Union could not compete with this new level of technological development that it could not afford. Thus did the Cold War pivot from mutually assured destruction to mutually assured magical thinking.

On February 28, 1987, after two years under Gorbachev, the Soviets withdrew their objections to the SDI and announced their willingness to lead to reduction of both medium-range missile in Europe and intercontinental missiles. The Soviet Union was suffering from their economic slowdown due to lack of western technology and lowering of the world price of oil from Russian sources. Following the November 1986 summit, the price of oil continued to fall to the tune of $15/barrel from $30-40. The withdrawal of Soviet troops from Afghanistan occurred; it was seen in the haze of the post-Cold War victory, given the level of American support of the mujihadeen. However, Afghanistan was not Iran; it had no oil reserves. The zealots released by the American support had been trained to become the basis for the eventual quagmire it served to be for America,

By the third summit at Governors Island in New York in December 1987, Gorbachev agreed to the terms stated. The treaty was ratified by the U.S. Congress on May 28th, 1988. In his fourth summit meeting ending on June 1st, 1988 in Moscow, the Cold War could be said to end. In 1989, at a speech at the United Nations, Gorbachev announced that the Soviet Union would unilaterally cut its contribution to the Warsaw Pact by a half-million troops and 10,000 tanks without any Western *quid pro quo*. With Wall Street as a backdrop on Governor's Island in December 1988, the Soviet leader in effect offered his surrender to President Reagan and to President-elect George HW Bush.

President Reagan had been pushing against an open door. Gornbachev had left that door open by the state of the Soviet economy. At the beginning of 1989, the Soviet sphere of influence in Eastern Europe seemed as solid as anytime during the past forty-five years of history. By the end of the year, the Brezhnev Doctrine was dead; each country in the former Soviet bloc was going its own way. By the end of the year, what the Red Army had won in 1945 no longer existed. German unification could occur. It was the ordinary people who achieved it.

The existence of atomic weapons insured that war between the superpowers did not take place. The focus on this possibility ensured that the Cold War had its long duration. The Cold War may be remembered as the time when military strength as a measure of power itself for the past five centuries ceased to be that. The Soviet Union collapsed with its military power intact. The Soviet economy was in crisis and its hold on Eastern Europe could no longer be sustained due to loss of fear of Soviet power.

The Iran-Contra Affair

The lack of involvement by President Reagan in the day-to-day workings of his administration was highlighted in this fiasco. In November 1986, the details first appeared in a Lebanese newspaper that secret arms sales were being made to Iran, forbidden by Congressional embargo. These arms sales were made to members of the Revolutionary Guards to free hostages taken by Shiite forces in Lebanon. The profits from these sales were then being funneled via Colonel Oliver North of the staff of the National Security Council to support the anti-Sandanista "contras" in Nicaragua fighting the Ortega government. The sales to the latter were also forbidden by Congress.

President Ronald Reagan, a supporter of the contras, although evidence existed to the contrary, claimed that he was unaware of the diversion of arms to the contras. Several months later, after much confusion and lack of access to papers, the president admitted in March 1987 his "full responsibility" for the actions. It was only the president's personal popularity that kept his presidency alive. What was becoming clear that President Reagan was being protected; that there may have been other instances when his understanding had been compromised. More than a covert operation, it was a gulling of the entire population. The country could not believe it was being lied to so brazenly.

As evidenced by the Iran-Contra controversy, President Reagan was fundamentally a "Teflon president" as though nothing stuck to affect him personally. His most powerful impact on social policy was his appointments to the bench. Antonin Scalia was a product of the Federalist Society, the belief that one should interpret the Constitution according to its literal wording and original intent. Scores of his other appointments to the lower courts were already at work reversing decades of liberal drift. President Reagan appointed nearly four hundred to the federal bench.

Tax reform was his most important intervention on behalf of the working poor. He lifted six million off the tax rolls and expanded the earned income tax credit. He signed the act giving amnesty to three million undocumented aliens. After the 1986 election when the Democrats increased their Senate majority, he supported welfare provisions sponsored by Senator Moynihan. The Family Support Act significantly increased welfare spending in return for increased incentives for work. Most important was the shift hat occurred in foreign policy between the first and second terms. Both the hardliner and the peacemaker were present but the balance shifted from one to the other to appear to be a discontinuity.

President Reagan offered an olive branch throughout as he also raised the ante. Since the rise of Gorbachev to power, he finally found a Soviet leader who could respond to his oft-expressed wish to commune directly with a leader able to do so. He was aided in this direction by Secretary of State Schultz and protected him from Secretary of Defense Weinberger and William Casey of the CIA who opposed nuclear disarmament. Another less well known influence was Suzanne Massie. An author interested in Russian culture, she conveyed to the president a deeper knowledge of the ordinary Russian; the one he addressed in his wish to cut through the Soviet bureaucracy.

Riding a horse in Mexico after he left office, he was finally diagnosed at the Mayo Clinic with Alzheimer's Disease. Protected by his wife, he was never again seen in public in his diminished state.

The Legacy of Ronald Reagan in Washington

Most inappropriate is the Ronald Reagan Building International Trade Center in the Federal Triangle. It had been named for him to get Republican support for this long awaited completion of the set of the Federal Triangle that had been aborted as a result of the

Depression in the 1930's. The most expensive federal building up to its date in 1998, it belied the political tradition that represented his stance for reduced government expenditure.

President Reagan had succeeded in changing the attitude toward the government, for better or worse. His popularity and accomplishments restored the idea that someone could indeed be successful in that job. At the same time, he insured a hypocritical attitude toward Washington. It was as though it could cost less but do more. Farmers continued to demand farm subsidies; the elderly their Medicare; homeowners their subsidized mortgages. Deregulation and pro-business policies provided opportunities for the unscrupulous to take advantage. But we clearly don't want much government.

CHAPTER 9
THE GEORGE HERBERT WALKER BUSH SUCCESSION 1980-1984

Introduction

Figure 40 - George Herbert Walker Bush

George Herbert Walker Bush was born in 1924, the second son of Prescott and Dorothy Bush in the cloistered world of the moneyed Eastern Establishment. His mother was a leading women's tennis champion who raised him to be a "gentleman." He grew up in Greenwich Connecticut, his father the son of an Ohio steel executive and son-in-law of an important Wall Street investor; later in 1952 a Connecticut Republican U.S. Senator. Young Bush entered Phillips Academy at Andover at age twelve where he was considered "charming" and never defiant to even the most authoritarian teacher. He enlisted in 1942 when he turned eighteen, the first in his class. A naval aviator, he was rescued from a downed plane. Post-war, after Yale and the ancestral Skull & Bones, he moved to Texas to found his own fortune with Dresser Industries, a subsidiary of this father's firm. His motto was "make some money so that you can serve."

In October 1987 at Houston Hyatt Regency Hotel, George H.W. Bush announced his candidacy for the presidency to the tune of *The Yellow Rose of Texas*. He would give the nation the benefit of "steady and experienced leadership" as the successor of President Ronald Reagan.

Settled in Midland Texas, he cashed in on the oil of the Permian Basin. He made his first million based on the Zapata Oil Company financed by his Uncle Walker's money while reduced to bragging that he loved eating "pork rinds." Bush found his home in Houston, a prime site for the budding Texan Republican Party. The region's social conservatism and fundamentalism were united to laissez-faire capitalism nurtured by the oil industry "derring do" tradition, He ran for office in a newly formed Republican Congressional district in Houston in 1966, serving for two terms. After failure to receive the Republican nomination for senator, he was given by President Nixon the job as U.N. Ambassador. In the wake of Watergate, he then took the thankless job as chair of the Republican National Committee before going to China. The last was a reprieve from the Washington wars post Watergate.

On his return, he was given by President Ford the opportunity to once again serve, in the name of duty, taking on the job as Director of the CIA, then under fire. Finally, after withdrawing from the presidential run in 1980, he met Ronald Reagan's requirements to oppose abortion and run as his vice-president. Now having become President Reagan's man, Bush performed as expected. Never one to dissent, he chose to admit that he was "not in the loop" to deal with the Iran-Contra fiasco.

The likely Democratic candidate, Governor Dukakis of Massachusetts had carried out a frugal administration. Lee Atwater, the Bush campaign manager, had been reviewing the Dukakis record. Willie Horton had been convicted of murdering a teen-aged service station attendant. Sentenced to life imprisonment in Massachusetts, he had nevertheless been given a weekend furlough. Making his way to Maryland, he killed a man and raped his fiancé. The furor had aroused considerable interest in Massachusetts but Dukakis had been reluctant to end the furlough policy and did so only in 1988.

Massachusetts was unique in permitting lifers to receive furloughs. In actuality, during its decade of existence, the program had only four out of 268 convicts escape while on furlough; only one had committed a crime. Aiming at Reagan Democrats, this particular case was clearly a winner for Bush's campaign. Well aware of the racial overtones, the decision was made to use the case of Willie Horton in a series of TV ads, attributing to Dukakis the entire responsibility for its decade of existence. Disclaiming responsibility for its distribution, the Bush campaign had been clear to Lee Atwater that the goal throughout the campaign to make Willie Horton a household name. He succeeded in making the voters more fully cognizant that Dukakis was indeed "soft on crime."

In order to deal with the "wimp" image, Bush would spend thirty minutes before each encounter with the press with Lee Atwater to "buff himself up." It was agreed that the campaign would be the most slashing presidential campaign since that of President Harry Truman in 1948. Dukakis failed to emphasize Bush's elite background; he also failed to emphasize the changes for the course of the rich during the 1980s as well as the bankruptcy of the working class that had occurred. George H.W. Bush won with 53% of the vote and overwhelmingly in the Electoral College while still losing seats in the Congress.

The End of the Cold War

On the accession of George H.W. Bush in January 1989 as the successor of President Ronald Reagan, the Cold War was still far from over. Gorbachev's "glasnost" and "perestroika" were designed to increase the efficiency of the system, not to increase democracy but to maintain power. Soviet troops remained in Eastern Europe; Germany remained divided. The Warsaw Pact was intact. The goal of the NSC Director Brent Scowcroft, trained in the Cold War, remained to maintain stability, to serve American interests and be helpful to the peaceful cessation of Soviet domination of Eastern Europe, end the division of Germany and to end the Cold War - all without violence and war.

Figure 41 - Brent Scowcroft

Brent Scowcroft was born in Ogden Utah in 1925 of Utah Mormon parentage. He graduated from West Point in 1947 and joined the U.S. Air Force. He had a variety of additional training opportunities including a doctorate in 1967 in International Relations from Columbia. He carried out a variety of posts at the Pentagon and the Department of Defense before joining the White House staff as deputy to Henry Kissinger during the Nixon and then as Director of National Security under President Ford. Long associated with Henry Kissinger, he later joined the George H. W. Bush Administrations as National Security Director.

The close friend of President Bush, Scowcroft was cautious. Fearful of a crackdown like that of Hungary in 1956, the Americans remained wary. Poland, under the aegis of the Polish-born Pope and with the Solidarity Union was the leader. The test of 1989 was whether it would be the dawn of a new era or foretell the return to Hungary of 1956. The new era was not merely anti-Communist; it also foretold of East European nationalism. Moreover, what would be the implications of a reunited Germany?

Scowcroft saw it as essential to move liberalization forward while meeting the limits offered by changes in the Soviet Union so as not to put Gorbachev in a corner.

In a speech in May 1989, President Bush announced the end of the process of containment. By preventing further expansion, the United States had succeeded in having the Soviet Union face its own inhumane and inefficient system. What was the wave of the future was a world "in which democracies anchoring international peace and a dynamic free-market system generating prosperity and progress on a global scale." There was not the breath of vision to meet what was indeed the opportunities offered.

The response to the protests in Tiananmen Square in Beijing was far different from the response to Eastern Europe. Both President Bush and Scowcroft welcomed cooperation with the Chinese Communist Party and economic liberalization without the need to encourage political liberalization. From the start under Nixon, the focus had been to bolster China as a partner vis-a-vis the Soviet Union; not to liberalize the plight of the Chinese people. There had been a clear understanding that the aim of China's leaders had been to prevent decentralization and to avenge their sense of western infringement of Chinese territoriality in the 19th century. Somehow, it had always been understood that the economic liberalization in the form of an approximation of a free-market economy would inevitably lead to political liberalization but the connection was never spelled out. Hence, there was handwringing but no clear cut American interest in the fate of the students in Tiananmen Square. Scowcroft saw American interest in economic stability and political interests in East Asia that he reinforced in the course of two trips to Beijing during 1989.

During the fall of 1989, demonstrations and mass exodus of East Germans continued to flow through Hungary. Finally, the Berlin Wall fell just days after the celebration of the 40th anniversary of the German Democratic Republic (East Germany). President Bush refused to "gloat." "I am not an emotional kind of guy." It was essential not to humiliate the Soviet Union and create another Versailles Treaty syndrome. President Bush encouraged Chancellor Kohl of the German Federal Republic (West Germany) to move ahead for reunification in the name of "self-determination." The reunited Germany remained in NATO; Russia agreed that to maintain Germany within NATO to the exclusion of a Germany as a free agent within Europe.

The break-up of the non-Russian components of the Soviet Union then proceeded. Lithuania was a case in point among the Baltic states annexed by the Soviet Union on the eve of the Second World War. The pre-Second World War government had been permitted to maintain an embassy on 16th Street in Washington DC since 1940. In March 1990, Lithuanian nationalists declared independence in Vilnius. President Bush reiterated the stance taken for self-determination without making any public statements. The year 1989 was indeed a miraculous one but what had happened was not met with much response by the White House,

Nationalism also took hold in the former Soviet Union. Many of the non-Russian elements such as Belarus, the Ukraine as well as Kazakhstan, Georgia, and Uzbekistan all left with the Great Russian heartland remaining alone. By the summer of 1991, these forces continued to destabilize the Soviet Union and Gorbachev appeared to be doomed. On August 19th, 1991, the coup occurred. With Yeltsin in control, Gorbachev eventually resigned on Christmas Day 1991. President Bush had successfully dealt with the demise of the Soviet Union so as to carry out its demise without a shot being fired. What was to be expected from a future Russia? Was it to be a resurgent nationalism as Gorbachev was threatened? One thing that clearly needed to be dealt with was the safety of the nuclear arms residing in the non-Russian vestiges of the former Soviet Union. The Senators Nunn and Lugar bill dealt with such protection.

The Gulf War

In August 1990, the forces of the Iraq leader Saddam Hussein invaded the emirate of adjacent oil-rich Kuwait. There had been long standing disputes between the two countries but the major one dealt with the debts incurred by Iraq in its war with Iran. Saddam Hussein had considered his role in the war with Iran to be consistent with the needs of his neighboring oil producers. Sales of oil by Kuwait had been seen to undercut the price of oil to the detriment of Iraq's balance of payments. It was thus far from clear that Kuwait was a benign actor. Nevertheless, the NSC Director Brent Scowcroft insisted that Saddam Hussein should withdraw and persuaded President Bush to agree.

The danger was not merely inherent in the action taken but the portent of further actions that would severely complicate further

American interests in the crucial oil region. The so-called Doctrine issued by President Carter had defined this area as crucial to American interests. Much of the daily usage of American oil came from imports; almost all of Japanese and other foreign friends were dependent on foreign oil Although oil was the issue, President George H. W. Bush insisted that the issue was that of aggression on poor little Kuwait. It is not surprising that the Bush family found their interests rooted in the Midlands section of West Texas somehow connected to the oil interests of the United States.

American interests included the preservation of oil shipments from this area with particular attention to the safeguarding of those of Saudi Arabia. During the eight previous years, there had been a war between Iran and Iraq that had ended in stalemate. Iraq under Saddam Hussein had invaded Iran to grab some of western Iran alongside the border with Iraq. The Iranian forces had fought back albeit with great loss of life. It took some fancy footwork but Saddam Hussein was no longer designated as an enemy. His forces had been well supplied by American arms during his war with Iran.

Once and again Secretary of Defense Rumsfeld appeared in Bagdad to show support. American and other western, as well as Soviet war materiel was sent to prop him up. This became what was to be used in poison gas attacks during the Iraq-Iran war as well as those used in attacks on Kurdish civilians within Iraq. Saddam Hussein had amassed one of the world's largest armies in the interim.

Invoking the principles of Winston Churchill vis-a-vis the appeasement of Hitler, President Bush was steadfast in his refusal to accept the invasion. The Security Council, with what was now crucially available Soviet concurrence, supported the formation of a coalition to cause withdrawal. A new world order was in the offing. With the Cold War over, the dream of FDR for a new world via collective security in the UN could come about. A military solution was also in the offing; approval was sought from Saudi Arabia for a quarter-million American troops to land there in preparation to back up sanctions. The king of Saudi Arabia agreed to permit a large-scale non-Muslim force to enter his country the Land of the Holy Places.

In accordance with the "Powell Doctrine" of Army Chief Colin Powell, military efforts were to be large enough in scale to carry out the task with a clear endpoint and clear exit strategy. The Viet Nam syndrome would need to be overcome. That is, American military power would be used; and used freely. "Desert Shield" was the name of the operation to protect Saudi Arabia from invasion. The Saudi king was shown Iraqi troops massing on their border. There was an agreement for American forces to come to Saudi Arabia.

Contributions to the coalition were to be made by Arab enemies of Iraq such as Syria, Egypt, as well as Saudi Arabia. Financial contributions were solicited not only from Saudi Arabia and Kuwait but also from Germany and Japan, the latter particularly dependent on Mid-East oil. Britain and France would contribute forces as well, reluctantly as part of a UN force. President Bush was acclaimed for his skill in amassing such a multilateral force. Israel was studiously excluded in order to maintain an Arab force. The CIA had also been unleashed to increase its efforts to subvert Saddam Hussein within Iraq.

Economic sanctions had been imposed by the UN to insure withdrawal. An ultimatum had been issued for withdrawal from Kuwait by Saddam Hussein by January 15, 1991. He refused. The effort now extended not only to expel Saddam Hussein from Kuwait but also to inflict enough damage on his forces to reduce their potential for future aggression.

The election of 1990 had intervened. The Republicans lost nine House seats as part of the Great Taxpayers' Revolt. Moreover, President Bush vetoed a civil rights bill in his lead-up to election to allay his base. With the 1990 election already complete without any significant change in Democratic Party control, on the day after the mid-term election, President Bush ordered an enlargement of the forces available; calling for the reserves and National Guard necessary. The issue remained as to the need to seek Congressional agreement for the American forces already being placed in Saudi Arabia.

Sanctions did not have a chance to work but preparations were already in place for invasion. Invoking Saddam Hussein's already well-known use of poison gas and nuclear interests, and despite the protests of his Secretary of Defense Dick Cheney, President Bush nevertheless pushed for a vote "for the use of all necessary force" to implement the UN Security Council resolution. The vote in Congress came on January 10th in the House prior to the more reluctant Senate. It seemed hypocritical to many in Congress to require approval for the extensive actions already taken. It was difficult to not support the troops already in place to invade. The need to invade was pressing due to the coming hot weather. Ten Democrats joined his close majority supporting the president in the Senate. Although reluctant to do so, the Legislature had indeed taken up the challenge to carry out its Constitutional duty.

"Desert Storm" started on 17th January 1991. American TV viewers witnessed an unprecedented display of high tech military capability, carried out by an air-war by the coalition organized by the Commander-in-chief President Bush. It was D-Day, without the casualties; so different from the Viet Bam War that had been carried out with the constraints that limited American effectiveness. The war's political goals were limited to ouster of the Iraqi forces from Kuwait but now appeared to be enlarged. At his State of the Union speech on January 29th, President Bush once again cast the war as part of the American destiny. "We are Americans...For two centuries, we've done the hard work of freedom." The military goals were somewhat larger; to include the destruction of Saddam Hussein's Revolutionary Guards in the process of their ejection from Kuwait.

The nation was on the verge of the next American century. The attacks thus far had nullified the Iraqi Navy and Air Force and done extensive damage to infrastructure. Ground troops would be needed to drive Saddam Hussein out of Kuwait and to limit the capability of Iraqi ground forces. On the 24th of February, the ground war began. Within hours, the battle was over. It was a "Hundred Hour War" in which the death toll was so lopsided that less than 160 American soldiers were killed while there were 150,000 Iraqi soldiers killed. Its endpoint was vague, yet the Viet Nam syndrome had been cured.

The goal must be for Saddam Hussein to be deposed by some sort of internal military coup. However, the Turks were pleased that Iraq remained to keep the Kurds under control; the other Arabs also thought it necessary to keep the Shiites under control. Iraq had been put together by the British after the end of the First World War; it would continue for now. Saddam had not been destroyed after all; nor had his biological weapons nor apparently his nuclear capabilities been affected. They still existed to awaken other efforts.

The New World Order

The letdown after the Gulf War was enormous. President Bush had called what he had done the "start of a new world order." Both the Soviet Union and the United States had collaborated to make it possible for the UN to take the lead. The election of 1992 was pending. President Bush did not like "the money thing." It was the "ugliness of the press, their carping." that made him feel miserable. Once more, before Gorbachev's fall, there was the signing of the START Treaty that provided for the mutual destruction of ICBMs and missile warheads. Any effort to support Gorbachev was looked at askance by the Republican right.

Although President Bush was seen to be clearly in charge in terms of national security, the economy was failing. Even Kevin Phillips, the harbinger of the Nixonian Republican majority, joined those who noted that the poor were suffering while the rich had gained in those last years of the Cold War. The ghettoes of American cities grew; drugs grew apace and education failed. President George H.W. Bush, who had vetoed a civil rights bill, offered no remedies to meet the challenges. The large number of blacks in the Gulf War American military reflected the lack of opportunity for such blacks elsewhere in civilian life. President Bush seemed impatient, bored by his job.

Was it possible that to entertain the notion that the world had become more precarious, not less so, now that the end of the Cold War had come about? If the disappearance of the Soviet Union had removed one threat, others had taken root. Nationalism and religious fundamentalism became more apparent. The Gulf Adventure had harmed the nation because it diverted the country from its basic internal problems. The DOD budget remained high, hovering around $350 billion (in 2015 dollars). The legacy of the Cold War transformed the nation, making it less moral, less innocent and, only superficially more motivated to address its fundamental social problems.

It has been noted that the country, in exercising global leadership, continued to maintain military capabilities staggeringly in excess of that required for self-defense. In the wake of the Second World War, an affinity for military power emerged as central to the American identity. The five decades of the Cold War had ended but there was no possibility of emerging from the current era of myth and fable. The

Gulf War had merely re-enforced it. It had established the myth of the American hero in the form of President George Herbert Walker Bush safeguarded the poor female figure of little Kuwait from the rapacious evil of Saddam Hussein. Stability in the Persian Gulf could not be guaranteed by the victory that had been secured.

The idea that the American presidency was a casualty of the Cold War was not something discussed in the corridors of the White House. FDR mobilized the country to share the products of a self-confident society. He asked for sacrifice from millions during the Second World War. He recognized the importance of engaging the public in their dreams for the future. Among the fruits of the Cold War were the secrecy it has generated; the "dirty tricks," it had justified; and the illusions it had propagated.

Indeed the President of the United States held the fate of the world in his hands; that his finger on the hands on the button gave him considerable power. Even into the 1970's, the work begun under President Franklin Roosevelt enabled the presidents of either party to accept the premise of the twentieth century liberal project. The Republicans might occasionally slow the expansion of government but never challenged the premise that it was the only way address society's greatest challenges in the 20th century.

President Ronald Reagan challenged that assumption, but could not as he had claimed to have done in his 1981 budget, to "have boldly reversed the trend in government."

However, the country was infantilized by the Cold War. White House staffs, and the new multi-tiered federal bureaucracies guaranteed that those who served the president would indulge him in his fancies and fantasies. The multifaceted intelligence apparatus is ultimately responsive to political interests of the Executive.

Congress was seen as an appendix that sought only to impede the hard working and self-important members of the Executive. Their concern with local jobs in the defense industry and campaign contributions from defense industry made them pliable. The White House became the only show on earth, the small city on the Potomac suddenly elevated to be the center of the universe. By 1990, the deficit he had inherited from President Reagan had grown so large that his successor President George Herbert Walker Bush had to raise taxes in what had been the largest tax increase thus far. The voters had long preferred President Reagan's talk of "Morning in America." President Bush's party revolted, contributing to his loss to Bill Clinton in 1992. The problems of the Middle East remain to haunt future presidencies.

The country President Reagan left behind was quite different from when he took office in1980. He led the way in the direction the country was to go in the successive years. The notion that government could lead the country, acting deliberately and collectively, and can address our common problems, was ridiculed. The very capacity of government, through raising taxes, was weakened. The only capacity of government was to enable the already powerful to seize for the already powerful an even larger amount of the wealth produced and control those who are left behind.

President Ronald Reagan was the last of the men who led the United States during the half century starting in 1941 under his then idol of FDR. The country has become more confident but also more selfish; better at generating wealth but much worse at distributing it. There was growth but also greed. Like his early hero of FDR, Ronald Reagan became president when the future looked bleak. He raised its morale through both a set of policies and a reassertion of national values. He led the United States to be the global victor in the battle of ideas vis-a-vis Communism. He believed that the United States was everywhere a force for good in the world. When it succeeded in such, it represented the best part of the role of our country in this, the American Century.

THE END

LIST OF FIGURES

WORKS CONSULTED

Ambrose, Stephen A. *Nixon. The Education of a Politician* 1913-1962 New York: Simon and Schuster, 1987.

Anderson, Martin and Annelise Anderson. *Reagan's Secret War*. New York: Crown Publishers, 2006.

Barone, Michael. Our Country. The Shaping of America from Roosevelt to Reagan. New York: The Free Press, 1990.

Basevich, Andrew. *America's War for the Greater Middle East*. New York; Random house, 200116.

Bernstein, Mark. *McCulloch of Ohio. For the Republic*. Crow Equipment Corporation, 2014.

Berkowitz, Edward D. Mr. Social Security. The Life of Wilbur J. Cohen.

Lawrence, KS: University Press of Kansas, 1995.

Bingham, Clara. *Witness to the Revolution*. New York: Random House, 2016.

Bornet, Vaughan. "Reappraising the Presidency of Lyndon B. Johnson" *Presidential Studies Quarterly*. v.20 (Summer 1990) 591-602

Brands, H.W. *Reagan The Life*. New York: Doubleday, 2015.

_____*The General vs the President*. New York: Doubleday, 2016.

Brauer, Carl M. "Kennedy, Johnson and the War on Poverty" *The Journal of American History* v. 69 (June 1982) 98-119.

Brinkley, David. *Washington Goes to War*. New York: Alfred A. Knopf, 1998.

_____. *The End of Reform*. New York: Alfred A Knopf. 1995.

Busch, Andrew E. *Truman's Triumphs*. Topeka: University Pres of Kansas, 2012.

Califano, Joseph A. Jr. *Inside. A Public and Private Life*. New York: Public Affairs, 2004.

Caro, Robert The Years of Lyndon Johnson. The Path to Power. New York: Alfred A Knopf 1981.

_____ *The Years of Lyndon Johnson Means of Ascent*. New York: Alfred A Knopf, 1990

_____ The Years of Lyndon Johnson. Master of the Senate. New York: Alfred A Knopf, 2002

_____*The Passage of Power.* New York: Alfred A Knopf, 2012

Conkin, Paul. Big Daddy from the Paternalism. Lyndon Baines Johnson. New York: Twayne Publishers, 1986.

Dallek, Robert. *Lone Star Rising. Lyndon Johnson and his Times. 1908-1960.* New York: Oxford University Press, 1981.

_____Flawed Giant. Lyndon Johnson and his Times 1961-1973. New York: Oxford University Press, 1998.

_____Nixon and Kissinger. Oartnrs ibn Power. New York: Harper and Row, 2005.

Davis, Michael D. and Hunter Clark. *Thurgood Marshall.* New York: Carol Publishing Group, 1992.

Donaldson, Gary. The First Modern Campaign. Lanham MD:Rowland & Littlefield, 20025

Dumbrill, John. *The Carter Presidency. A Re-evaluation.* Manchester, Englnd: Manchester University Press, 1993.

Dunn, Charles W. American Exceptioionalism. Lanham, MD: Rowman & Littlefield, 2013.

E#hrenreich, John. *Third Wave Capitalism.* Ithaca, NY: Cornell University Press, 2016.

Ehrman, John. *The Eighties.* New Haven: Yale University Press. 2005

Evans, Rowland and Robert Novak. *The Reagan Revolution.* New York: E.P. Dutton, 1981.

Finch, L. Boyd. *Legacies of Camelot.* Norman: University of Oklahoma Press, 2008.

Fink, Gary B and Hugh Davis Graham. *The Carter Presidency. Policy Choice s in the Post-New Era.* Topeka, KS: University Press of Kansas. 1998.

Fischer, Beth A, *The Reagan Reversal.* Columbia, MO: The University of Missouri Press, 1997.

Fitzgerald, Frances. *Way Out there in the Blue.* New York: Simon & Schuster2000.

Gaddis, John L. *The Cold War. A New History.* New York: The Penguin Press, 2005.

Garrettson, Charles L. III. *Hubert H. Humphrey. The Politics of Joy.* New Brunswick NJ: Transaction Publishers, 1993.

Giglio, James N. *The Presidency of John F. Kennedy.* Lawrence KS: The University Press of Kansas, 2006.

Glad, Betty. An Outsider in the White House. Jimmy Carter, His Advisors and the Making of American Foreign Policy. Ithaca: Cornell University Press, 2009.

Goodwin, Doris Kearns. *Lyndon Johnson and the America Dream.* New York: St Martins 1976.

_____The Fitzgerald's and the Kennedys 1987

Goodwin Richard. *Remembering America. A Voice from the Sixties.* Boston: Little, Brown & Co., 1988.

Graubard Stephen. *Mr., Bush's War.* New York: Hill and Wang, 1992,

Greene, John R. *America in the Sixties.* Syracuse: Syracuse University Press., 2010

Hoffman, David E. *The Dead Hand.* New York: Doubleday, 2009.

Isaacson, Walter. *Kissinger* New York: Simon and Schuster, 1992.

.Johnson, Haynes. *Sleepwalking Through History.* New York: W.W. Norton and Company, 1991.

Jones, Alan M. "Nixon and the World." In Alan M Jones, Ed., *U.S. Foreign Policy in a Changing World.* New York: David McKay Company, 1973.

Achenbach, Nicholas *Some of It was Fun.* New York: W.W. Norton, 2008

Kalb, Marvin and Deborah Kalb. *Haunting Legacy.* Washington DC: Brookings Institution Press, 2011.

Katznelson, Ira. *Fear Itself.* New York: Live right Publishing, 2013.

Kinzer, Stephen. *The Brothers.* New York: Henry Holt and Company,, 2013.

Kissinger, Henry. *World Order.* New York: Penguin Press, 2014.

Korda. Michael. *Ike. The American Hero.* .New York: Harper, 2007.

Maddow,Rachel. *Drift.* New York: Crown Publishers, 2012.

McCartney, Jmaes with Molly McCartney. *America's War Machine.* New York: St Martin's Press, 2016.

McCoy, Donald R. *The Presidency of Harry S. Truman.* Topeka: The University Press of Kansas, 1964.

McCullogh, David. *Truman.* New York: Simon and Schuster, 1993.

_____*The Wright Brothers.* New York: Simon and Schuster, 2015.

Meacham, Jon. Destiny and Power. The American Odyssey of George Herbert Walker Bush. New York: Random House, 2015.

Morgan, Evan. *Nixon.* London: Oxford University Press. 2002.

Nelson, Craig, *The Age of Radiance.* New York: Scribner, 2014.

Newton, Jim. *Eisenhower. The White House Years.* New York: Doubleday, 2011.

Parmet, Herbert S. *George Bush. The Life of a Lone Star Yankee.* New York: Scribners, 1997.

Patterson, Thomas G. *The Origins of the Cold War.* Lexington, Mass: D.C. Heath Company.

Perry, William J. *My Journey at the Nuclear Brink.* Stanford, CA: Stanford University Press, 20015

Phillips, Kevin. T*he Politics of Rich and Poor.* New York: Random House, 1990.

Reardon Steven. "Paul Nitze and NSC-68" in Anna Kasten Nelson Editor *The Policy Makers* Lanham, MD: Rowland and Littlefield, 2009.

Remini, Robert V. *The House. The History of the House of Representatives.* Washington, DC: The Library of Congress, 2006.

Reedy, George. *Lyndon B. Johnson, A Memoir.* New York: Andrews and MC Meel, 1982

Rorabaugh, W.J. *Kennedy and the Promise of the Sixties.* New York: Cambridge University Press, 2002

Rulon, Philip R. The Compassionate Samaritan: The Life of Lyndon Baines Johnson. Chicago: Nelson-Hall, 1981

Saull, Richard. *The Cold War and After.* London: The Pluto Press, 2007.

Savage, Sean J. *Truman and the Democratic Party,* Lexington, KY: University Press of KY, 1997.

_____ *JFK, LBJ and the Democratic Party.* Albany: State University of New York Press, 2004.

Schmidt, Karl M. *Henry A. Wallace, Quixotic Crusade 1948.* Syracuse: Syracuse University Press, 1960.

Schmitz, David F. Brent Scowcroft. New York: Rowan & Littlefield, 2011.

Shoup, Laurence. *The Carter Presidency and Beyond. Power and Politics in the 1980's*. Palo Alto: Ramparts Press, 1980.

Siderenko, Konstantin. *Robert F Kennedy. A Spiritual Biography*. New York: The Crossroad Publishing Company, 2000.

Smith, Curt. *George H.W. Bush. Character at the Core*. Lincoln NE: The University of Nebraska Press, 2014.

Smith, Jean Edward. *FDR*. New York: Random House, 2008

Solberg, Carl. *Hubert Humphrey. A Biography*. New York: W.W. Norton Co, 1984.

Sorensen, Ted. Counselor. A Life at the Edge of History. New York: Harper, 2008.

Stebenne, David. *Arthur J. Goldberg. New Deal Liberal*. New York: Oxford University Press, 1996.

Stein, Jean and George Plimpton. *American Journey. The Times of Robert Kennedy*. New York: Harcourt Brace Jovanovich, Inc. 1970.

Stern, Mark. "John F. Kennedy and Civil Rights. From Congress to the Presidency" *Presidential Studies Quarterly* v. 19 (Fall 1989) 797-823.

Stossel, Scott. *Sarge. The Life and Times of Sargent Shriver*. Washington, DC: Smithsonian Books, 2004.

Strong, Robert A. Working in the World. Jimmy Carter and the Workings of American Foreign Policy. Baton Rouge: Louisiana State University Press, 2000.

Thomas, Evan. *Being Nixon. A Man Divided*, New York: Random House, 2015.

Thomas, G. Scott. *A New World to Be Won*. Santa Barbara: Praeger, 2011.

Thompson, Nicholas. The Hawk and the Dove. Paul Nitze, George Kennon and the History of the Cold War. New York: Henry Holt and Company, 2009.

Thurber, Timothy. "The Second Reconstruction" In Zelizer, Julian *The American Congress. The Building of Democracy*. Boston: Houghton Mifflin Company, 2004.

Vance, Cyrus. *Hard Choices*. New York: Simon and Schuster, 1983.

Weiner, Tim. *One Man Against the World*. New York: Henry Holt and Company, 20015

Weisberg, Jacob. *Ronald Reagan*. New York: Times Books, 2016.

Wills, Garry. *Reagan's America*. Garden City: Doubleday & Company, 1987.

Woods, Randall B. *LBJ. Architect of American Ambition*. Cambridge: Harvard University Press, 2006.

INDEX

ABOUT THE AUTHOR

Mark N. Ozer As a professor of Neurology at Georgetown University Medical School, the author had a productive career in medicine. After retirement, he returned to his first love of history nurtured as an honors graduate of Harvard College. A resident of Washington since 1964, he has translated his interest in that city into a series of books: *Washington, DC: Politics and Place* (2009), *Washington DC: Streets and Statues (2012)* and *Washington Metroland* (2013), *Washington DC and the War of 1812: Like a Phoenix from the Ashes* (2014), *Washington DC and the Civil War: The National Capital* (2015) and, most recently *Washington DC, The National Shrine: 1890 - 1940.*

At the Osher Lifelong Learning Institute at The American University, he taught concerning the interaction of history and geography of many of the great cities of the world. Among American cities, in addition to his explorations of Washington as both a City and Capital, there has been *Baltimore: Persons and Places* (2013), *Boston: Persons and Places* (2015), and even more recently, *Philadelphia: Persons and Places* (2016).

Thanks to Lynn Kasdorf for his excellent work in book design and editing.

See www.markozerbooks.com for a full list including E-books

69836630R00123

Made in the USA
Columbia, SC
24 April 2017